polalka

Karolina Zapal

Spuyten Duyvil
New York City

Library of Congress Cataloging-in-Publication Data

Names: Zapal, Karolina, author.
Title: Polalka / Karolina Zapal.
Description: New York City : Spuyten Duyvil, [2018]
Identifiers: LCCN 2018014053 | ISBN 9781947980532
Classification: LCC PS3626.A638 A6 2018 | DDC 811/.6--dc23
LC record available at https://lccn.loc.gov/2018014053

Dedicated to all immigrants, migrants, travelers, and off-breeds whose home is language motherlinear.

"An extraordinary cavalcade of poetry comes into being: through the force of adult imagination, the poet who began as a divided child forces together precisely what would tear him apart. In this way the poem itself provides a shelter for the homeless mind."

Meena Alexander

"All we can do now, in the wake of this intolerance, is take care of our corner. And our corner may change. This year it actualizes in Boulder, Colorado. Next year, it may be (inter)national."

Shawnie Hamer, in a parking lot at 1am

Contents

- -

A note to the reader: roman numerals indicate the presence of an endnote correlating to the text. The endnotes assume the form of letters shuffled back and forth across the ocean. It is possible to read them with movement as they are meant or all at once, upon completion, as if they comprise the contents of a singular envelope wading into pools with different addresses. Be warned, a dotted line will solidify through speed and frequency of correspondence, but a hyphen, though connecting two wor(l)ds, will not make a third.

_____

Introduction

My parents immigrated to the United States from Poland through the Diversity Visa Lottery in 1994, a year after I was born. Because they hadn't acquired a place to live, a car, or a job, they deemed it necessary to handle matters alone; their heightened sense of responsibility as emigrants from a reduced country influenced their decision to leave me behind. Consequently, as they set off for America with two suitcases each and a lack of livable language, I encroached on my grandparents' privacies. For six years, I replaced my mother as my grandmother's child, becoming the subject of her gatherings and letters.

Because my parents hadn't taken me with them initially, their only choice was to file an I-130 Petition for Alien Relative form, thinking it would take a couple months to process, which perfectly matched their timeline for settling into factory jobs and a Chicago basement. The petition filed in 1994 finally processed in 1999, falling victim to an incessant backlog of I-130 applications, the number of them far exceeding the number of visas allotted in a given year. I entered this sky-scraped geography five years late, a month before starting the first grade.

In *Stigmata: Escaping Texts*, Hélène Cixous says, *One must enter the labyrinth of a text with a thread*, not unlike the spool of red I received in Sunday school as a child, the one metaphorically attached to Jesus at one end. I fell hard into America, leaving behind a thread that has over the years pooled and knotted in the space between my past and present self. Similarly, when readers tie a loop around their waist and jump in, they cause the affixed gas station nozzle to peepukecumcryspill on their shoes, into their tanks, their capacity to go. Readers confirm stories based on their chosen imaginations. They are the biggest influence when it comes to what comes.

The thread that electrifies these pages receives its volty and ampy—*cute* synonyms for scientific words—from a migration that started at birth, yet didn't transport my physical body. Everyone knew I was in the process of leaving and felt at liberty to discuss my new home. During religion class in kindergarten, the priest compared my upcoming journey to those undertaken in the Bible. *Will you forget?*—sails unfurled over the open sea.

My extended family and I lived in a leaving economy: a tiny farm town a couple hours south of Kraków, next door to one another like ducks in a row. Except we didn't have our ducks in a row. My grandparents owned one of four cars in town, purchased with my grandfather's cleaning up after the Vietnam War, meaning with a blast that invalidated his ability to hear in one ear. Day after day, he drove women in labor to a hospital occupied by doctors who cared for their patients only when paid extra under the table, and back to a secular cloister fit only for inland mermaids. Family structure standardized: wife tended to the home, and husband worked abroad for months at a time, visiting only to bring back meager pay and a dose of his sperm, funding another child to tend. Although the number of families who emigrate as a unit has grown, back then my parents were an anomaly. Or two-thirds an anomaly.

In a common physics analogy involving water, *current* means flow, and *voltage* means pressure. Here, the thread flows through a comforting muchness, looking to guide, but also pressure, familial memory governing a country never in its own hands. Polishing regards Poland in the same way italics regard Italy—barely; the colors vary, & I beg in

You're always So Sleepy You're always So Sleepy You're always So Sleepy You're always So Sleepy

You're always So Sleepy You're always So Sleepy You're always So Sleepy You're always So Sleepy

You're always So Sleepy You're always So Sleepy You're always So Sleepy You're always So Sleepy

You're always So Sleepy You're always So Sleepy You're always So Sleepy You're always So Sleepy

You're always So Sleepy You're always So Sleepy You're always So Sleepy You're always So Sleepy

You're always So Sleepy You're always So Sleepy You're always So Sleepy You're always So Sleepy

You're always So Sleepy You're always So Sleepy You're always So Sleepy You're always So Sleepy

You're always So Sleepy You're always So Sleepy You're always So Sleepy You're always So Sleepy

You're always So Sleepy You're always So Sleepy You're always So Sleepy You're always So Sleepy

You're always So Sleepy You're always So Sleepy You're always So Sleepy You're always So Sleepy

You're always So Sleepy You're always So Sleepy You're always So Sleepy You're always So Sleepy

You're always So Sleepy You're always So Sleepy You're always So Sleepy You're always So Sleepy

You're always So Sleepy You're always So Sleepy You're always So Sleepy You're always So Sleepy

you're always so sleepy you're always so sleepy
you're always so sleepy you're always so sleepy
you're always so sleepy you're always so sleepy
urinal weight socially p urinal weight socially p
urinal weight socially p urinal weight socially p
urinal weight socially p urinal weight socially p
jutro wariaty sosna lipy jutro wariaty sosna lipy
jutro wariaty sosna lipy jutro wariaty sosna lipy
jutro wariaty sosna lipy jutro wariaty sosna lipy

picking up women
from the hospital after they've given birth I did it five or six times I did it
one time I laughed so hard I almost stopped the cccooooooooooooooooo   CCCC o
one time from the hospital I laughed so hard I almost stopped the car
we were halfway home from the hospital
almost stopped the coooooooooooooooooooooooooooooo
the man turned to his wife and asked what did you give birth to
he hospital when I almost stopped the cooooooooooooooooooo
we were halfway home from the hospital when this mother $#@%^&   asked what the hell
was in the backseat of my CCCC o   I laughed so hard I almost stopped the cooooooooooo
stopped the coooooooooohhhhhhhhhhhhhh
CCCC o   even I knew it was a girl

- *immigrant*: exotic
- *child of immigrant*: exception to subsequent points
- *teenager of immigrant*: neighborhood walks the neighborhood in a neighborhood stroller as if around a doll neighborhood
- *adult of immigrant*: ugly and deformed a neighborhood styled from the consecutive travels of one person the roofs sounding like barks because really they're rooves like missing grooves and whose on overworked hooves and hives and his

- *an excerpted child of exotic immigrants*: having been born in polepohleohlholeand and committed to America like a crime at age six now at age twenty-four I undulate between and hole when I babysit it's not my baby it's not my baby it doesn't dare
- *immigrant of immigrant*: every traditional Polish name for a girl ends in a he's on and she's ona always tagged with a always a abstinent a abducted   they a beautiful oni a commanding I aз
- *immigrant moth*   rom my erotica
  because I ke   language but
  promise I ca   autocorrects
  to foreign   so be it

- *child of im*   Pierce) yes
  I would lo   anspire just
  breathe I w
- *teenager of im*   doesn't come
  through well on   nsistor then OK
  yet sleeping on frie   string of tantrums
  and you're not suppose   just amplify them
- *adult of immigrant*: raised as an imp for inopportune because I thought of that before impossible and as a result doesn't know how to deal with the
- *gimmick of rent*: to stay in one place is to

- *immigrandkid*: grandma's trying to explain where she's from and it's like explaining good to a child using only one-syllable words good is farm and town but not sit-tea is name but not my-name all love is good hug kiss sex heart the love good is bye
- *grand teenager*: grandma tags a teenager yes OK fornicate but baby explain my abstinent language which would I rather be that's easy dent or found yes we are in need of more evolution
- *adult*: trying I of on to make ion make couches of an immigrant make tourists of an immigrant yet still cannot decipher between transit or transistor which would I rather be that's hard sit or stor

I

"The immigrant is seen as exotic, but the offspring ugly and deformed, except when a child. The neighborhood teenage girls want to walk you around the block in a stroller, as though you were a doll, which gives you reoccurring nightmares about being kidnapped. They want to strip you of your clothes [when you are twelve] in a utility room where no one will see. In this unkempt sentence, in this lattice of vagueness, lies violence." (Pierce)

Immigrant: exotic question. Marked solely by retaining mother tongue. Noun. Fatherland's key witness to immigrants' facing survival after sustaining blows of monochromic synchronicity. Redundancy question. Marked by wholesome literate America. Why is language motherly question. Marked by tongue umbilical cord that feeds crescent-slopes from the throat's placenta to the back of the placenta's throat. Really just interprets history to know language learns from the mother. But it's no longer true question.[1] Marked endangered twice. The flavor of the tongue of course but also the flavor of the mother. Passes her religion to her children just like that, but shouldn't there be a test? My Jewish partner worries I'll pass my Catholicism to our children like a terminal illness, entongueing, entitling, entombing each one in a matronly inception. I don't have an accent; therefore I'm not possessive over my children's faith nor exotic but maybe paper-thin. A fragment of exoskeleton allied with the real animal. Especially at the zoo a question.[2]
 Marked by holey literature &

---

1 "I forgot [her] word for 'fog.' I had memories of this city, that much I recall, a city from my former life that I don't choose to name now. In this city it was raining. 'At last you're mine,' I called" (Dutton).

2 ...of which side takes me for belonging(s). That we're separated by cages makes it clearer, but then, the real animal and I both commit our presence to the same ocean-side.

Exotic? Solely by having retained mother tongue, yet cannot noun since her functions convert to verb.[3] Converbs: sound, talk, accent become *to* sound, *to* talk, *to* accent. The mother tongue and mother constantly fluctuate. When I am six years old, Polish attempts to pronounce *noh-oohn*, no-noun. It's a verb. Don't you feel it in your mo-uth?

New language tells rules[4] to (de)(in)form skin with their barbed nails. Collects indents[5] to write bigger things. Exile recess

brains / reassess exiled brains

allied with the real animal.

Holey literature & I like it there.

3 The only true nouns are those that, as part of their meaning operations, perform only as nouns, like beauty. One cannot verb beauty without adding an if: beautify.
4 Rules as parasites as para, meaning beyond, sight.
5 i.e., tabs.

Holey literature, noun:

Written by half-breeds whose parents are different countries. *People with holes in their breeding* is literature that's not safe from the wind. Society forces half-breeds to patch up their holes, Americanize their breeding, especially in the telling of stories. Yet birds do not adapt their song to location, as chirpy and off-tune as it may be.

Half-breeds write their forces, stories, holes, change their stories from off-tune holes. Literature forces song on location, off-tune by off-breed who tells its holes.

Except, in migration,

many songs

go unsung.

A doll, a letter, a coat, some money, a letter, some winter letter boots. My parents send my grandmother a letter. She sends them letters of the alphabet they forgot.

English doesn't parallel their absurd physical choreo-geography. They send them back, having no use

for letters.

On my eighteenth birthday, they hand them over in a faded brown envelope:

here is the childhood we experienced.[i]

I don't want to strip you of your mother tongue, just around your tongue because I worry you'll pass your grandmother's writing, make language motherlinear.

Grandmother, do you sound like a terminal illness?

Child of immigrant: the foreign child epitomizes cuteness from a distance and readily welcomes friends and language. Although maybe I don't do this with grace. The commotion of twigs, thirsted mulch, and scavenged cloth that guts provisional earth caps composes the playtime of my survival. Lifting first energy through the dirt, we bypass domesticated play. *Chase me! Cię means you*, but why are *you* running away? We stand in solidarity against the fifth-grade boys who kick our nests and squeal.[6] Swallow anguage, though it feels like a nest going down. To catch what used to wear eccentricity on my tongue, a lack——of accent marks like seatbelt clicks clipping letters. And those missing from my new alphabet. Without pause, replace the wow-y ł in my last name with the nearest accessible stiff. This sacrifices zaPOW. Raise my hand for a turn at answering yellow means slow down[7] and further questions of girlhood. Print my name Karoli-a-na on my U.S. passport. Zapal. The actual Polish command for *light this on fire*. It's a mistake &

6 Not entirely true, or rather, incorrect in its totality; we stand in solidarity, yet this does not exert itself beyond solid. Airy—out in the open—it is only when a boy comes to our defense by casting a punch that teachers notice and meet with those "involved" while the girls stand on, watching.

7 The first question I hear and answer in English, which earns me a bright orange double-tiered ruler. My classmates stutter and stomp until the teacher brings them identical rules the next day.

We live in a leaving economy. We leave in a living

economy[ii]

Undulate between a hassle learner and what we call ESL.

Crouch-half-slouch haphazardly scooting down the wall on a slippery Winnie the Pooh backpack,[8]

wailing:

please police

   prosze prosie.

   They make jokes, don't let me please.

When I don't understand, the teacher calls in the same dictionary and so the same phlegm.[9] He performs it so easily, this English in English.

Roots kiss cry-chewing gum as adhesive. A nest going down to catch what used to wear eccentricity. And hold them.

In high school, he spots me playing tennis near his apartment and introduces me to his thick mug of preferences: kissing smiles and detoxified roots. He says, *I thought you were pretty even then* with roots smothered in medicine. I was your tranapist, translator-therapist, like every boy when spreading a nest. You tainted my third grade with choking cheeks owed to slow progress: learning *Wednesday* (memory) learning *necklace* (memory), but this shared history is as uselessly harmful as chewing gum in the gut.

He spreads a rumor I jerk him off with my eye sockets, my protective brother jerks. It's a mistake to give up my name. With fire I throw fire & I don't cry like that anymore.

---

8 "It was raining on the grass. The reflection of a rainbow was rubbing up the wall" (Dutton).
9 From Greek, *humor caused by heat.* A half-black childhood friend can't stop laughing after she learns the Polish word for leg, noga. She cheers leg leg leg until it mutates to glug glug glug.

Diary entry, 2010, 17 years old:

A made me laugh today. We took a practice ACT in physics, and this one problem on bobbing golf balls or something kept asking about the period of bob and the amplitude of bob. *A* actually went up to the teacher and asked who Bob was. *A* said he thought he was essential to the question.

"American youth of Polish descent thrown into the swirl of life here must make use of their English language. They can no longer isolate them-selves by forming their own groups like their parents did who came from beyond the ocean." (Jaroszyńska-Kirchmann)

Bob is inevitable when walking a sunny trail bitten by shadow at the margin. Paper trail bitten by shadow at the margin   alias.

You are bob, but here's some advice for the immigrant: for the rest of your life, pretend you're Bob, so you can be essential to the question.

Sometimes it's fun to joke. *Daj mi loda* means both *give me ice cream*
and *give me a blowjob*, but other times I want to stay in my woods,
in my single meaning of wood, which is hard when I know two lan-
guages to quadruple meaning,

and people say,

Let in only one language,
        a trench code to the floor.

Grandmother, do you sound?

Like a terminus—either end of a railroad line.
Your daughters find safety in movement.

Teenager of immigrant: neighborhood walks the neighborhood in a neighborhood stroller as if around a doll neighborhood. While the officers arraign our drug addict neighbor, they contemplate ringing our bell, but won't. Offer congratulations on our upstanding citizenship. What does it feels like inside of what it is? Big city suburb of this high country. Cun try to escape this bullyhole, this holebully theatric of language in a public school, where everyone strives to be one or a couple. I learned English for *this*? I come first unless I'm fifth. Up to elbows in romantic numerals I II III. IVow to show the neighborhood girls my poetry. They say, *Right you don't have capital there*, pointing to my vocabulary. They release the stroller, and as it hee-haws over able-bodied roots into a stream of consciousness, they ask, *Where is the master going? But here's a stick to chase you with*. It's called the ugly stick &

I.

Having returned early from a return to Poland, Mother and I dread sleeping in the house alone. Without my father, we're not alone. It happens on a Wednesday (memory) at two a.m. in a doll neighborhood streaming pristine plastic streets. A car crashes into nearly every recycling bin on the block, screeching to a halt after each confined obliteration. Through cupped hands, the street appears benign, knocked only by an entering wind. And then it happens. The driver returns for round two thirty, hits the ones he missed. Did I say plastic? I mean place and stick because I'm still in the mindset of recess, what it feels like inside of night what it is.

Ten years later, at the same window, Mother and I gaze at a curious light swinging from a tic-tac. Father laughs at us, says, *You and your UFOs*. He cups his hands to see what they shop in a doll neighborhood. Please, police, we aren't a loan.

II.

A Polish flag dangles on our front porch as a shield of honor or cor-
rection, sure, but question protection, question the day I come home
from school unaware of the felled patio table bleeding in a million
gashed shards, and later when my parents notice it first, they blame
me until someone starts leaving rags in our front stoop nests.[10]
They curse, *Who would do such a thing to birds*[11]
but ultimately retire the flag with exaggerated casualness expressed
by folks' restoring string lights to their intended season. When I
dream of home, I dream of Poland, even though I've lived for nine-
teen years. A flag lag. I'm an age, and there's an egg stewing there.

Birds smell the migration and settle

                                                    for the memories.

---

10 Maybe those equipped with rag(e) thought: "Very small birds frighten me, flying at my eyes as if to a region of
brightness split into bands" (Chapman). An immigrant family settles in suburb-culture or sub-culture—a region
of brightness.
11 "Our gaze reveals that nests are not safe"(Chapman).

III.

The neighborhood girls beat hips refusing to infinity boys because of their misinformed coordination, beat boobs refusing to hang attractively close to traffic because of their impossibly small size, beat vagina refusing to handle the jaw-seat of a rollercoaster because it's a docile diaper. You're not a woman if you can't grind and show off your tits and take a good cock. It's called the ugly stick & I look like a lipstick, a swollen bathing suit.

"But our youth, interacting with Americans, assimilates their traits, and in order to achieve and win their respect, disown their Polish nationality. This is to some degree unjustified since in order to win respect and esteem from Americans it is not necessary to be an American." (Jaroszyńska-Kirchmann)

Necessary to be a neighborhood girl walked there by the neighborhood football star who buys me a freshly squeezed lemonade and asks a billion questions because I'm intriguing, different. Googling the Midwest, I'm meta-euphoric. He tells me I'm interesting only in his status. He's interested only in, concerned with, my status.

It's not meta if the place doesn't dream.

It's research.

I'm bullied on the school bus in first and fourth grade. The seats are landlocked, and I'm an island. Crashing on the underbelly of my best friend's gum-pebbled sneakers, I take my parent's advice and make her a star

chart. Each day I arrive home safely, I seal a sticker shut. Up in her first home with the football star and baby at twenty-four.

One of these things is not like the others.

You don't think you have an accent? You do a little,
like a pickle to a cucumber.

Adult of immigrant: ugly and deformed. A neighborhood styled from
A neighborhood styled from the consecutive travels of one person,
the resulting roofs sounding like dogs because really they're roofs,
like missing grooves and who's on overworked hooves, and hives,
and his &

Legend:

They want capital, my capital.

Warszawa / Wars zawa

Longitude is positive and America, negative.

From the perspective of a negative photograph,
where the light appears darkest, and dark, lightest:

Wierszawa. *Wiersz* means
poem.

Excerpted child of exotic immigrants: born in polepohleolholeand and committed to America like a crime at age six, but why does it take so long to open the hole, to o pen the hole, or cover the port (a potty) hole with straw, deceiving the sight yet not the stink? That's the crime. Being eastern is synonymous with earstern because yes, I'm here to listen, not to talk. The first time I hear my voice I am twenty-two hiking with my blind roommate: *step over here, watch out for this thing*. Describe, please advise. Talking in thises and thoses, yet working on my thesis. Who's this advisor those ad-visa? At the mercy of violent input system America. No children in the exit row, even if that means they're separated from their parents, even if they're separated form. Driving to a college interview after years of mutual misjudged cues about our relationship, my father tells me the only thing he regrets even now is leaving me in Poland. Worried about money, worried about two suitcases and a basement apartment with a baby. Idealized case(ment) forces us apart. They petition the U.S. Citizen and Immigration Services to please reunite them with their child, but the turnover rate for children is a kind of joint pain. Visage renews to visa age, and the mad wait on petitions plots reasons for relocation, what for ripe personhood now just a body. Airplane, you carry aliens, yet people apprehend UFOs—*ufam ci*—on overworked hooves, and hives, and his & I'm a sheep pronoun in the beehave.[12]

---

12 All animals zdychają (die), except for the horse and bee that umierają (pass away). They die by euphemism. We have to respect the horse's mouth and the bee's knees. To beehave is to die by euphemism.

Their first home in America, a child's nest crackling under the weight of a rock, the wait of me the smallest igniting igneous rock. Chicago, '94. When I ask them about it, a long face summarizes vertigo and sweeping mutterings of luck. Then a memory follows, that of sharing a bathroom with a Russian immigrant. Then a memory unfollows, cooking there. Deflated by the question, they say they must have eaten. It must have rained on them like on the gums of a boiling teapot. All furniture on credit—money to buy the suburbs. They keep only two spongy, brown chairs I frame in my *un-memory*[iii]

and forget to cap a message-a-bottle in

a transitory environment,   so the
bottle
drowns.

The following information pertains solely to the Chicago district but counts petitions from every nation. My parents file for alien relative (I-130) in 1994. At that time, the backlog of pending I-130 applications at year end is 781. The backlog of *all* pending alien applications at year end is 16,056 This only worsens with time. In 1995, the backlog of pending I-130 applications at year end is 2,352, and the backlog of all pending alien applications at year end is 51,335. In 2000, the number for the previous is 13,746 and the latter, 84,454.[13]

Years I. II. III. IV. V. *"What sex is the 'I'..."*[14]
when it stands before the capital V then loses to it?

VI.E

translates to *ubiegać się*, the word *run*.

Simultaneously run yourself and cave to desire.

---

13 "If language...reaches the state of a pure equation...the writer becomes irretrievably honest" (Barthes).
14 The quote continues: "Does one have to believe that God is a Woman to say 'I' as a woman and be writing about the human condition?" (Sontag).

My name reaches the front of the visa line,[15] stabs the center of attention &

negative turns to

n   elk grove   ative

n   ~~EG~~   ative

n   ative

The suburb I'll live in for the next twelve years.

*"A very important matter for the Polish children in America is to ac-
quaint them, if only by letters, with children in* Poland[iv] *"*

(Jaroszyńska-Kirchmann)

15 Zapal is to light on fire, and *zapałka* (Zapał, Ka-) the word for a match. This, scrambled, *złap*, is the word for catch, a ball or an illness. Catch up, on the other hand, is *dogonić*—the consecutive travels of one person the resulting roofs sounding like dogs.

PREFERENCES

Family	All Charge-ability Areas Except Those Listed	CHINA-mainland born	INDIA	MEXICO	PHILIPPINES
1st	15FEB98	15FEB98	15FEB98	08AUG93	22AUG87
2A*	22DEC94	22DEC94	22DEC94	22NOV93	22DEC94
2B	08JUL92	08JUL92	08JUL92	22JUL91	08JUL92
3rd	01AUG95	01AUG95	01AUG95	08NOV90	01JUL87
4th	22JUL88	22JUL88	15AUG86	01APR88	15JAN79

United States Department of State Visa Bulletin for June, 1999. Listed are priority dates (dates of I-130 form completion) that have finally reached the front of the visa line. It takes until this bulletin in 1999 for my parents' priority date to show (circled). Family 1st concerns children of citizens. Family 2A, my category, concerns children of permanent residents. The priority date for category 4 for the Philippines shows a 20-year waiting game for brothers and sisters of American citizens.

Family-Sponsored	All Chargeability Areas Except Those Listed	CHINA-mainland born	INDIA	MEXICO	PHILIPPINES
F1	01JUN10	01JUN10	01JUN10	15MAY95	15DEC05
F2A	08MAY15	08MAY15	08MAY15	22APR15	08MAY15
F2B	15AUG10	15AUG10	15AUG10	22NOV95	01MAY06
F3	22APR05	22APR05	22APR05	22DEC94	08SEP94
F4	22FEB04	22FEB04	22JUL03	01JUN97	01AUG93

United States Department of State Visa Bulletin for March, 2017. Oddly, the applications for children of citizens (F1) appear more backlogged than those for children of permanent residents (F2A), resulting in a five-year difference in reverse. For brothers and sisters of American citizens who currently reside in the Philippines, the wait has increased to 24 years.

"An approval of an I-130 petition only means that your relative can file for an immigrant visa...does not give your relative any rights until the CIS or a consulate officer interviews your relative and makes a decision on whether or not your relative can become a lawful permanent resident." (Visa Journey)

If men are divisible by V

rip rip rip rip rip

                          done to you is   *done.*[16]

Is it during this interview that some man-adult with expired partialness asks me, *Will you be a good girl in America?* And I study his flat, sun-chapped picnic bench and answer, *Yes I'm here to listen, not to talk?* Maybe he responds with the same pride that compresses moths with important documents when they flutter unforgiving in his white. Open wombs shatter windows and God too, so be a good one and cinch the blinds for security because whatever casualty's done to you is exposure. Of course I don't remember details, only that I complain monotonously of hunger until my grandmother buys me an *obwarzanka* from a tourist cart.[17] Doesn't fail my current effort to redact the man's smirk, *nothing to worry about here boys,* and those boys' glutted humors as each one through the years commands some form of *behave yourself* from the young female behind the counter who wishes simply for a stamped passport and portpass through the airport gates. Now ask, *Do you wish to be a good woman?* You can choose the definition, and I answer, *Yes I'm here to talk.* It sways me eastward on a sinning wind, but at least I'm windy (still).

---

16 "If men are divisible by five./ Rip, rip, rip, rip, rip./ Done" (Tolbert).
17 I may be remembering the event of petitioning for a visitor's visa, rather than the formal immigration interview, because they denied me. My grandmother dispatched fury—how could they refuse to bend the rules for a child separated from one's parents? Blasphemy! Boredom and blasphemy!

Voice a vice with a mOuth until I move to *Colorado*[v] and fall into step with a blind woman whose disposition overturns her ocular muteness.[18] *Aren't you here to be a writer? You sound unfunded and far.* Smoky voice disconnects from vocabulary, voice too weak, voice too slow, too voice! Now I can be sure at least a naked droning[19] backs my friends' fibrous stories, important opinions. I stab the center of attention & walk my bike down and force my body through its spokes.

Sometimes I meet the tall city with a fist and other times with a to-do-list I can only accomplish in the rain when the mood's just right for motivation bred from forgiveness.

I love you too, Poland, but I must hope, not fear,

some man-adult with indistinguishable birth certificates from heaven.

18 "Note that the word 'mute' (from Latin mutus and Greek μύειν) is regarded by linguists as an onomatopoeic formation referring not to silence but to a certain fundamental opacity of human being, which likes to show the truth by allowing it to be seen hiding" (Carson).
19 "It was a kind of nakedness, a feeling of nerve endings in the wind" (Jamison).

Separated form, which am I? The bottle cap, the bottle, or the message? I fear I am entering a riddle: they walk into a bar; some poor thing points *ten* for an English dentist, and ten of her teeth are gone in the form of a subliminal message. Lips uncap. Tongue-bottle spills out. A dream of serving interim on city council turns to a retraction of voice in fear of firing a debate that inflames anyway. *I couldn't have started it*, I wail, and Professor says, *Yes but you didn't defend yourself, either*. The perfect sound abandons a sore throat and plops into a tin of already expended gargling oil.

My parents have coffee with America's ego, and what's more emotionally than ego, the bird? *Dziennik Związkowy* open to name name name, year after year, morning after morning. Dew sees less repetition. Still nothing and no sleep till the right z broods that putrid night. For the longest time I assume it's because I'm about to enter the first grade (America wants to lock my education in a binder, maintain it with tax money), but when I ask my father, he charges it to coincidence.

When America catches wind of national tragedy—bridge-crossing, indistinguishable spell of *crowds* and *cowards*—it rings a cluttered tune: a cat reggae-crying, no, a warning system splaying. She's a warning system playing. She's only a child; we have enough *time*[vi]

Only when I become legible, I become legal eligible.

The officers process me with my back throwing forward my back, throwing forward my belly swelled with tax money. I assume I'm a baby of fortune, but I'm only a copy of fortune, paper that means nothing with its ink.

Finally aboard this retreat from dying,

                                        it's only a copy of me.

I need help with my capital, my vocabulary.
Pluvial: it means *like rain*.
Oh, so like my hair, pluvial in your,
in your
mouth,
just like that.
Pluvial may be a copy of the weather, forming from its absence.
You hold this thin fortune. It means nothing to hold me.

Everyone YEARNS a green card, sometimes YEARS a green one.

Water touches the green card holder. It's my mother, and when cows eat too much clover, their belly swells with a carnivorous ink, an exploring green ready to go exploding. Yet the farmer's smarter; in an effort to control his most valuable resource, he pours buckets for hours because water takes. It takes wet time in the hourglass to reach the United

shit; it goes like:

water takes out $\wedge$ flush takes in $\vee$ retreat of relatives who can fly.

For a time-discount, the immigrant may enter the number of rela-
tives with a dying

                                      petition
or the watered-down coffee that's all of a sudden not   watered
down. It takes years to feel the caffeine. You eat   it like a
pair of scissors for a   tongue,

but for scissors to paper,
a surcharge. To cut in line, do time or
bail.

Let go when it
lets hang, when it
legs, when it dries
and browns like a good expensive antique. The immigrant is the last
copy of real-relative with a hard-life. Coffee paper is seemingly more
durable than its too-bright counterpart.
Let go. *Tęsknota* is dangerous.

Tęsknota is nurturing a phantom fever in a friend's recliner, feeling only my pajama-shirt-dress undress because it's soft, but the jeans are numb, the bra, numb; they're part of my body. The water heater broke in my apartment, so I'm here at midnight, researching, *Is he real-friend or dream-friend?* The football star is also friend. The water heater broke in his status and also my tranapist. If I keep dreaming, they become real dolls for me to dress undress, but it's the opposite with home. The longer time dreams of place, the farther from that place I lose the yellow-orange stucco and three sweeping floors in the country HOME HoMe Home home hom om O. I lose the exactitude. It becomes part of my body.

In dreams I feel the length of the way more than I feel the way. The length is sensation.

Poem, 2009, 16 years old:

I am from a European country,
a place where pizza is a delicacy,
and the letters Q and V do not exist.
I am from military time and supper,

from a house that extends into the sky
like an overly flexible neck of a giraffe.
A wooden three-person swing stands guard in the front yard,
protecting me from boredom.

I am from a traditional Polish kitchen,
where my grandmother makes *pierogi*, *naleśniki*, and my favorite,
czerwony barszcz z uszkami.

I am from bus rides to the city,
a worn out place where cars are rare,
from black cats, superstitions,
and an opera of dogs singing me to sleep.

I am from real Christmas trees
and a goofy uncle pretending to be Santa Claus,
from chickens clucking and the sound
of church bells whenever anyone reaches the gates

of heaven.
I am from the seven p.m. cartoons
that wish me goodnight long before I'm ready
to sleep.

How does visa uphold in a country that disavows the letter v? The rule that declares who can fly...is a,

causes a kind of dying, like a flame biting the last inch of liquefied wax. Alien relatives anticipate relocation, their eyes focused on in-comprehensible sightings of wealth. Marriage certificate; prior-divorce papers; passport style color photo with the name *lightly* printed on the back; documentation exhibiting *co-mingling* of finances and laundry; birth certificates of any children involved; affidavits re-assuring the validity of someone's else's voice, a memory; affidavits reassuring the validity of the romantic partnership, explaining how the person acquired one's knowledge of your marriage: *yes, they ambled into my practice after her miscarriage. They said it was better this way. They wouldn't have to raise a baby on two continents,* Parent Trap *style with a real-twin and* dream-twin[vii]

At a family party, a man announces he's importing his partner to the U.S. and has hired a lawyer to help him through the process. The lawyer tells him, *The most provocative (proactive) way to yield romantic credibility is to acquire a joint life insurance policy.* At the party, incredulity reads on everyone's face. To place money on early love, on early life, is an illogical commitment, like wind agreeing to wear a vase. Years later, during a recession, Poland shines brighter. Someone else, more gossip. *What is she thinking? He won't want to move* here, to this legal Lego, a pre-determined structure on top of another, where jobs are as scarce as rabbits in the presence of a re-al-dog. She'll end up, no visa *required*[viii]

The website Immihelp helps migrants in proving bona fide marriage
by listing any number of privacies they can publish to really bond
find. Imagine truth like this having to calculate its perception—how
language renders a body perceived

versus

how that perception then renders a body lingual (perceptive).

> photographs of you and your spouse taken before and during
> your marriage
>
> wedding photographs, preferably those that include parents and
> other relatives from both families

(if the camera does not insert the date automatically, write the
date the picture was taken and a brief description on the back)
(do not take wedding or other videos; there won't be any time or
space to view them)
(the time that's broken only in that it refuses to break)

> copies of letters and/or emails between you
>
> phone bills showing your conversations
>
> receipts for gifts that you have purchased for each other
>
> copies of Christmas cards or other holiday cards addressed
> to you both

Are the officers who decide bona fide to the process, judging these
monotonous documents, or do they ask for a more entertaining set:
IV. a drug the body bills for confession / check
V. utilization of commonplace object in unsettling way / check
VI. both their genitals in numberical order / check mates
Four, five, six, pickup sticks IVVVI and place them

between two walls I I.

Polish Food Festival in Denver:

A friend urges me to talk to a man plump with strawberry fat who's running an immigration counseling booth. He urges and urgs and urgs and ur responsible for your art, which this interaction may inform. It is a day for lawyers to celebrate immigrants: a dollar per dumpling, a frame on auction for the ex-wife, and a beer, and a beer, and a hello, *dzieńdobry*? Hi? Urgent request to cut you open. A book is forming. What spires marriage in the office? Spires? Yes, the Latin *breath of life*. No, the English *conspires*. Yes, the English *aspires*. But he's a traditional wolf, and I'm a stone, replacing the foxy lady in his belly. *Ma'am, it costs twenty-five grand to fake a marriage, but here's a pamphlet*: LIVE CONCERT MEDIEVAL MUSIC A LOT OF FUN.

All USCIS requires of my mother is a copy of my birth certificate. That's the crime. For a child to file for a mother, solely a copy of the birth certificate, yet to file for a father, a birth certificate; a certificate recognizing that one's father was married to one's mother prior to one's birth; and evidence that an emotional or financial bond exists between the two. A man denied paternity because he enjoys an apple in his throat—what poisonous affection, what original sin. A baby out of wedlock can't bring him to America; a baby out of wedlock isn't his child.

Here's a man denied paternity because there's a body perceived. Here's a man denied paternity because he charges it for sustenance. Here's a *pan* denied maternity.   Eternity's implied.
          Nobody ever leaves.

Which is more important in the rendering of a certificate:
the mother tongue   the father   land?
One without the other,

                                    which comes first?

A nation can't stake claim without language,
                    but language has no basis without land.

When the aliens finally rise by chokehold, they actively corpse the Atlantic, an elastic body of wa(i)ter. Otherwise, passively, their barely viable bodies are expedited to a foreign grave. That's what's alien and grave where nobody leaves.[20] They rely on the chance mourner, otherwise lover, pressed firmly to the ground to wear them in to America. At a welcome-home party, the conversation's awkward because no one else thinks they're home. Emergencer! The outer space is closer than where we chart our fear of bury bodies. Parents of friends, friends of parents, pass before birds and ice water in the morning. I clock them Sunday-praying from one national emblem to another, the same predator bird who's identity-confused. The maids, the nannies, the truck drivers, hairdressers, unsuccessful, unhappy, not fluid in English, yet they stay. *We have kids in the schools*, they say, *In Poland, the math's different. The periods linger. 1.5 matches 1,5.* They plug for persistence. The comma winks at them; they wince. How can they be how it is to sleep in the *socket*[ix]

If it's heavy,   find the way back.

20 "1. 'Nobody is [emigrant].' 2. 'All trajectories are [psychotic] in their reliance upon arrival'" (Kapil).

For my father's aunt, it takes a stroke

in the water

     to return

to die.

           For my father, it takes my mother's begging

to stay,

to stay.

What dies within immigrants during relocation embodies a loved
one to have over for the holidays, a mirror's companion, a broom's.
And then it's impossible not to binge on what this loved one owns,
what she owes, in a fit of nostalgia on a brick sidewalk in the cold.
Both regret and hope.

Once, coffee smell at the bar so potent, at first, a fart. This makes me
queasy before I realize it's

a drug.

Someone has to tell them.

They come together, but what if they came apart?

Petal   felt   the whole flower crumbles.

What if Mother, what if Father, were a rose   apart?

They remember crackling on TV and stores stocked only with vinegar, remember the meat market dawn and ration papers for flour, chocolate, milk. One time my father brings home horse sausage just to prove to his family he waited in line. All that was left. A belly blistered from bread and instant coffee causes anxiety even now whenever camping threatens their surplus.

Does Mother ever come

together with him who picks salt off the screen, needles off a need less tree,

pining?[21]

.

She wins the lottery. My father, he's quiet. His plan to come to America, make bank (succeeds) and leave (fails). He pays mortgage to a fingertip instead of having built his own home on a fairy's back. Needle-less tree is a needy tree, is an unnecessary, unwanted tree.

Didn't Communism teach this?

---

21 "...People looking for an experience of radical dépaysement ['disorientation'], in which context they can give full vent to forbidden addictions (boys, drugs, liquor)...Communism—by definition—rules out the possibility of 'dépaysement.' No strangeness. (No alienation...)" (Sontag).

Does Mother ever rise,
rose? Has she raisin with someone
who takes

                                from where there is nothing left
to give?

          Does mother
tongue ever come
back to one so desperate for the sea
salt nourishment of the America
-n dream?
                              An immigrant moves as water
evaporates:
in vibrations caused by heat or as the extraction
          of sediment. Return is possible,

but only as rain.

Does he forgave for what she did or she forgive for who he is? For-
giveness shoots rain straight back to the sky. They'll wait, now, for
its return. Does she forgave or he forgive? And so it goes.

Preying on one emblem and another traces tears down a single bird's spine, Poland, the white, America, the bald. Together they generalize the deadpoet; *"The whiteness and wing span was awesome"* (Nobel). *Biały orzeł* is mainly a legend, a phlegm agent: brothers Lech, Czech, and Rus declare their father's kingdom too small to divide amongst themselves, so they wander Europe in search of a place to settle. Upon spotting the bird and considering it a good amen, Lech, with his vision, sets down his coffee and proceeds to lean entirely over the table to sip it. Oh open foam, oh frothy flames, grip my cheekbones and cause offense on my courtesy, for my neck is stronger than my arthritic hand. An elderly woman has the right idea: to sip backwards, it's piss, and there's a bowing involved to his brothers, Russia and the Czech Republic.[22] The town *Gniezno* (nest) and its companionship land contend for the most invaded country on the map. Only when Poland regains its independence do neighboring countries deliver the bird a crown, assuming it's *carrion*[x] &

22 Lech is the only one who doesn't assign his country his name. Instead, his name brands a rather popular Polish beer consumed today.

Beautifully brash and horny, yet simplified to white and bald.[23] Bald curiously holds record for the largest nest—a question of appearances. Do I shave for myself, or do I shave for America? I incur the largest nest from collecting a shedding

of immigrant status.

---

23 Unable to spring for double-headed, which describes the eagle in Albania, Montenegro, Russia, and Serbia's coat of arms, Poland and the U.S. keep it simple. On another note, America's eagle can be found in the Great Seal of the United States whereas Poland's eagle can be found in its coat of arms. Why does this, again, feel like Poland is subservient to the U.S.? It stands behind the U.S. in a long line of countries employing the eagle in exactly this manner: to protect. Not to vouch for, assign, or threaten.

On DCEagleCam.com, the following disclaimer can be found below the video feed:

This is a wild eagle nest, and anything can happen. While we hope that two healthy, juvenile eagles will end up fledging from the nest this summer, things like sibling rivalry, predators, and natural disaster can affect this eagle family and may be difficult to watch.

I don't know these eagles just like I don't know the actors who die in movies, yet this immediately arouses negative emotions—who, birds, do such a thing to birds? This applies to all narratives of immigration, as they involve familial strife for an interstitial audience. Seriously, read it again: while we hope that two healthy, juvenile humans will end up fledging, anything can happen. You're wild and foreign, yet a familiar narrative where anything can die.

Accipitridae, the family name for bald eagles, yet all I can think is: accent rips the day.

What's in language that isn't meant to live?

What's a symptom of language that outlives it?

                                        Accent,

an accident.

When it leaves,   ascent.

I do not sound like an outsider, and this scares people. I repeat my parents' orders to people with thick American ears. There's no hope for them, but I can say *th* and make lots of money.

All I'd have to do to humiliate them:
thread thumbs through three thick teeth
        in front of a large American audience.
                Repeat after me:
                        tread tombs true tree tick teef.

If everyone were Polish, this would be the funniest joke at the party.

Would I have sued immigration, the whole of it, if it had taken me a year later, after the accent cut-off? No, for something that would have helped

me belong &

To the outside.

In Poland, it's easy to belong elsewhere. People ask me if I'd move back, or how I'm settling in, or which country I like better. They sniff out the truth, even though I shoulder-nod an *I don't know*. When I'm a teenager visiting my grandparents, I'm taken to a hospital for an abnormally high fever. The doctor wants to keep me overnight for observation, treatment pending. Unsatisfied, my grandmother flashes my American passport, and it's enough for her to dose me with the strongest medicine and send me home. I feel better almost immediately. Later, I overhear my grandmother brag about this to my mother on the phone while I self-diagnose symptoms of a star, a star, an outsider who owes them.

But sometimes I am not based on my status. On the way to the hospital, a police officer stops my grandfather for speeding. Worried, he points to me in the backseat and says, *Please, officer, I'm only trying to get my American citizen to the hospital*. No, he lets go out of compassion.

II

"...making each man, if only for the scope

of one breath, something more

than a doll thrashed by need's reflex." (Hicok)

Immigrant of woman status: every traditional Polish name for a girl ends in *a*. He's *on*, and she's *ona*. Abstinent a, abducted a, abortive a. I dare you to find a name that ends in camouflag or space for us to rest. In English, *a* assumes an article with the headline: HERE IN aMERICa OUR NaMES aRE NOT GENDERED, which is most difficult to learn if born into classifying end

stop. You're a woman with womanly *a*'ss. They is *oni*, a mood that's awning on my tongue, wistful, protective, commanding *i* as the solution.

i means *and* in Polish.

Yes I, yes I, yes I

prepare a cup of decaf, let it cool, and fall asleep to the taste of...

introduce my mother to the thick of...

                                                 benign bitterness.

Without ever reading my writing, she says this shared history—
matrolinearly—is as uselessly harmful as chewing gum in the gut,

                                   where survivor's guilt

yes, but

        the English translation of *istnienie* is *no-no* (parts) or *exis-
tence* (equal the whole), and I choose to be

a part.

It's expected of every Polish girl who's on a first-name basis with tra-
dition to abstain from sexual conduct until marriage. It's expected
of her to oblige to ceremonious abduction of her will by a nice boy
from town who'll fart his sperm, worm to womb, recklessly suction-
ing a glob of caramel from a relentless hole. She's stuck, and he's
educating five beers after work with the boys. Lucky he's not the
one with vodka because the one with vodka leaves with it in his
head

       of breath,

                                                a contracting
uterus evolved to expel things that hurt & I've mistaken
masculine energy for sexual energy.

If I'm ever a bad girl, come home smelling
of woods or the trunk of a car,
        Poland blames America and America, Poland.
              Does everyone's blame accuse place,
take it poorly,
        especially when it's *wina*,   red and white?

The bottom floor of my grandfather's brother's home next door functions as a local convenience that oils men as often as women and their bread. The men, drunk, harass the bench that faces us with language and fluids that shouldn't a child. A property sin/tax: itching their crotch, jeering at women and their bred, laughing away their wife's requests to dilute their moth(er) crushing tone. Men own wo

men sing, *The girl loves us the girl utterus*—she's his (s)word. I watch them with intrus(t)ive eyes until I am old enough to realize they're staring too. Sight laden with judgment roosts on the balcony. Seduction soils itself and is due for a nap.

A male professor shows me doodles he conceives while watching his wife do housework. They are all men(tally women), and when I tell my partner and half-caf his response—*maybe they arrange-meant* (meaning marriage)—I reduce my ears to mere skins feeling ripped, pull the story of eye contact right from under us. It begins on a river-walk in Bilbao, where we clasp our hands to a normative whir-ring. The connection is free,

whispering   wifi, wifi,
wife.

The only *hasło* (or house to shut) we need is *e*, and the word in Polish is *żona*, the nearest to it I cuddle and seethe. The only zone we need is *e*, a half-open body to breathe &

Every Polish girl licks raindrops off clotheslines, begging for spirits to relieve her.

During pregnancy,
baby expecting women / *Baby* expecting men,
separated by contexts of giving
and receiving.
His genitals translate to a closed body, hers, she translates to an open window of insight, but anything open is an ad/vantage point.

They take it

and the cake too. With only a tractor to hide them and prime girl-walking hours to and from school, to and from church, to ig- or unite them, they train masculinity to weave matches into dresses until they're

dazzled,
dazed led.

They roughhouse on a grave marker, another, but their motives remain unclear. It's expected of man to have harmed or not; he's still a man, in that seduction downs itself and is due for another.

They pass out. Every woman

                passes them by,

                                but still, they get (a) head.

      Not everything's about sex.

No, it is.

      Nothing's going to happen.

Maybe, but I choose to carry myself in a backpack because my body

                        is everything,

is about *sex*[xi]

A man cannot stake claim without a woman,
                  but a woman has no basis without a man.

Immigrant mother[24]: I will not give birth to exotica from my erotica because I keep dating % love with great, and great, and great from Poland, just bright enough in memory to guilt this (my) delicate film of known (expended) ancestry. My partner cannot speak the language but promises I can foreigncate the children. That's a lie. For one parent to lack his children, especially the father who's not defined,[25] invites possessiveness and vengeance into the home. I refuse him his ancestor winter, seek vengeance on his great status. Foreigncate autocorrects to foreign *ate*, and if that's what it wants to be, a tourist, so be it &

My partner cannot speak the children, reminds me that because they do, they stain my woods (by staying my woods) whites and blues, so the sky's the same color as the fingers holding it up. My Polish language is no longer unique to me, but a spreading jelly of the off-poetry he likes, alien and relative, the lisp he adores.

24 "Who has not asked himself at one point or other: am I a monster, or is this what it means to be a person?" (Lispector). I write something about mothers, how they can't possibly feel monstrous after giving birth. But they look like monsters with a red gaping hole devouring in reverse. No longer having the option to punctuate (close).

25 "We wore a black sweater and you a plaid shirt" (Chapman). Woman forfeits individuality for collective warmth.

Hard Catholicism breeds the cycle: preying on praying on preying birds. But it's the same bird. My partner's right in that it's the same child. Making new children, separated from tradition, is like playing golf with the odds stacked against me. The holes are already there—I just have to score—but I cannot see them. So instead I wear a *golf* to collect a wisp in a glove. Pretend to harbor her forever instead of nine months, when suddenly she'll go

out

to play with the neighborhood girls of a different generation.

They'll dare her to exhibit
co-mingling of liquid and wax,
break the story down but also hold it
all together,

milk the past without draining its cow.

She'll carry an experience asking for contact,
                    each stone a person,
a city visited but untouched.

Her real-friend will inherit the archive of a migrant to her passing,
uncover an old candle, revive wax to an upward mobility, blow it
down, purchase another, shatter it glass-like on a cliff, but the whole
will still exist through sunlight's cradling the dead. It'll be different
with my daughter's living archive, inheriting something not because
it's dead but because it's afraid of death. Her friend will say, *It's about
our relationship, and the conflict is, she's dead.* My daughter will reply,
It's about our relationship, and the conflict is, no one can die.

But for all her talk of origin, she'll touch her ancestors only through
a great-great-grandmother   still *alive*[xii]

It'll be heavy,   finding the way back.

It's expected of every Polish girl to abort   abortion.

Legal only if the pregnancy stems from rape or poses a threat to the mother, but the Law and Justice Party known by its acronym PiS (to sip backwards) bids to save the fetus above all else, the bill backed by the prime minister—a woman whose name is a, as mine.[26] As a result, the flesh lot stinks of women fleeing, rather than their undeveloped sons, until they're trapped enough, old enough, to harm.

---

26 On October 3rd, 2016, and again on March 23, 2018, thousands of people in Poland went on strike against this total abortion ban in an event called "The Black Protest." As a result, the bill proposed by The Law and Justice Party did not pass. However, abortion remains illegal in most cases.

I cry at an American graveyard on a whim, my first, not whim. No one who dies for me dies for me here, but this cannot work in reverse: here does not die for me, does it there, and there, and everywhere else I'd kill to be.

My parents didn't want me to feel jealous of a baby from across the ocean. They were afraid I wouldn't want them, so really, they're selfish. They didn't have a, so they wouldn't lose two. Now he settles amongst American gravestones, shackling us to an empyre Zapal. Set fire to empires. He is not born and *I*[xiii]

The technician looks at the ultrasound, but the text appears foreign,

and when text appears foreign, we're inclined to implant our own thoughts as to what lurks on the page. What percentage of meaning depends on this secondary creation? I morph into a woman during sex who's willed into the role of her surroundings and cannot comprehend the estranged physicality of her body. Thus, she embeds the experience with thoughts about metaphorical sensuality and potent eroticism belonging to history. If pleasure depends on this translation, ultra-sound-art may work only when translated, too. A half-open body to breathe & I settle in city improper for all the dirty things this implies.

They translate me into a man. I am
a woman. To survive, I reduce my thoughts
to a normative whirring: look at the TV, cry at this book.
And then the whirring
stops. I miss you because everyone else is the same.

Lurk is the best way to tell people you're a immigrant with an inappropriate agenda. You can say it with anything: burgers, lettuce, casserole. They'll look at you as if you're a pre-dater

from the land before time, coming before a date, that's when. A dinosaur signs money orders for binoculars

into the future.

Authorization sounds like otherization, what they do when they help me belong & I wish there was a body that is not your body nor my body that we could touch each other through.

It's either a tree between us as we lay on the grass like babies, bicycling our legs (Conrad) or

when we inhale simultaneously and our shoulders brush from inflation.

OK Poland,   on *three*[xiv]

Body that is not your body nor my body
but a cat body we pass body
and forth. We're convinced he causes us
to dream more vividly:

we're crossing the Alps, paying five more of anything
because the village runs a popular path among tourists.

A body that is neither oxygen nor gender: oxygender, like a cleaning
product that costs five more of anything
because we're a popular kind of dirty.

Those who are immigrants,
those who wait/want to be immigrant,
those who are pushed into immigrancy/
                           infancy due to their physical-
i ty. And *you?*[xv]

This is a continuously morphing partner watch, but which two words are congealed by the hyphen-indelicate portraiture of gender? Continuously morphing partner-watch or continuously morphing-partner, watch! a show costing five less of anything. And me. Please hitch me on your continuously morphine. I think a mindset's thinning,

the lights are dimming.

Does it matter the angle

I'm seen? I write through Poland's binary canary, the color yellow with a white beak and bald cock, which decides: woman or guy, wick or gyroscope: *an apparatus...capable of maintaining the same absolute direction in space in spite of movements...?*

The world progresses but   •   does not.
Doll does not. Her views surrender to plastic corset died to plastic casket. Religion dances

only when moved by the one who plays it.

From a February 2016 post on Reddit:

hi im ° and i person
ally have identified myself as agender   i only came out
against me instead of respecting my gender
see the problem is   i live in poland
                          it's not 1
  its awful in this country
  i NEVER saw any other trans   ition
/non-binary person   in my (w)hole
          town   who doesnt wanna fit
no gender neutral pronouns in this language
i hate being   but i can get along with
masculine   pronouns always
but the problem is
no non-binary polish   sites topics or even single things
                                           for my family friends
and other   there is only a single page on Wikipedia in polish
                    NO information
to be considered
anything
besides "boy" and "girl" and she wanna cut my hair short but
                                              my parents dont allow me
could anybody help me   translations and other content to help me
silence

hi. im ida, and i personally have identified myself as agender for three years now. but i only came out to my closest friend. people seem to use it against me instead of actually respecting my gender. see, the problem is, i live in poland. in here, theres even gendered "me" and "i" and all that... its awful in this country. i NEVER saw any other trans/non-binary person in my whole town and beyond, and im super ashamed im the only one in this town who doesnt wanna be fit in the binary. i have decided to come out as soon as possible from on now.. but, there IS a problem that bothers me the most. there are no gender neutral pronouns in this language. only he/she/it. i really hate being binarised but i can get along with masculine pronouns, always. but the problem is, there are no non-binary polish sites, topics, or even single things that could help me explain it to my family, friends, and other people. on the internet, everybody knows im agender. but on the other hand, irl seems to matter the most. there is only a single page on wikipedia in polish but it states NO information about the gender, and it REALLY bothers me. i do not want to be considered female and NOBODY here knows anything besides "boy" and "girl" and everybody refers to me as a she. i wanna cut my hair short but my parents dont allow me, and lets not even talk about sex change. could anybody help me search for something about non-binary genders for polish people, or could provide some translations and other content to help me silence all of this? please, im begging you. ive been in the closet for the nearest 3 years and i come to hate myself and my body more every day. please, *help*[xvi]

First comment under the post:

I think you may have discovered your calling. If no one else is writing about transgender and agender stuff in Poland, it might be time to start. That being said, you should never feel obligated to put your health in danger. If you think it might be dangerous for you to write about this stuff, you might want to hold off until you can get out. There are a lot of less strict countries who are experiencing negative population growth and need educated people to move there. I think New Zealand is one of them.

The comment says you have to leave the dungeons to defeat them. If that's what it wants, a tourist, so be it & you'll stutter less when speaking in unisun.

Because

getting along with a white beak is what matters to be home.
        To foreigncate the same absolute direction requires
a different map.

But.

People have many primary identities,
                and the commenter forgets one of them is Polish,
so it's not easy to jump
corrections: your gender shouldn't have to be your calling, but it can
be. What matters here is safety *and* health.

Because

the canaries censor pages, so they can eye who's write and who the
pronouns no

But.

Write until your duty new zeal-ands.

Because

it is hard to write when the sun does not shine between your legs,
warming there—no warning there—because you're inside.

But.

I say, *Child of gender*: *"polycontinental transexperience"* (Pierce), yes,
I would love for my baby to but first for it only to transpire, just to
breathe, involuntarily for biology. Not like a child who craves atten-
tion and holds his breath in an appliance that washes it occasionally
till forced open by a hand.

What does it mean to wash breath?
Not for kissing but for swearing
off anger.

Because

plates and bowls clink in the government's machine. Platelets coag-
ulate. They stop the bleeding. Bowels seagullate. They break open
digestion-fish you're hiding for nourishment.

But.

Cells comprise your existence. The commenter cannot deny the dung(eon) smells in the place with the sun—a web spun in its light no longer a web, but a glass necklace. You may instead remodel *"... the odd converted garage of a cold room, how we string up the lanterns of our prayers, transforming the dungeon"* (Chen). In this old place, renewed, gag on language, gag on dongue, gag on giving, gag on plastic bags thrown inside wastebaskets. Of course females pass on singuvular qualities to their offsing, but only the male canaries sing. Gag them of their singing and come true for me, come truthfully, even if it's not by your own hand or that of trans/gression.

I have not once heard this word in Polish. It's implied. *Płeć* means *gender*, but if it escapes to America...

pleć with an *l* means

to braid.

I only came out to my baby because she's intimate
with the organs that produced her,
intestines flocking to life.

Human

violin, hollow body,

meaningful in its one-letter omission from *violint*, and, hey, this is
fun, creating absolutely whatever out of braiding

expectation[xvii]

discover   writing

        it might be   experiencing
    a   New

gender for biology

or

        need for educated people to have more than one identity—
New Zealand is a single identity.

Or

toast to female and beyond, Polish, and immigrant, and

beyond / *poza*.

Po means *after* and *za*, *behind*:   after behind,
            a toast to after the past.

No migrant should wear crayons to sleep, like a diaper catching the American dream, and wake with dollar bills' oils mounting the body. The sweat stinks, and money is nowhere in sight.

The bed does this, another's embrace uttersus or rudders: *device for governing*. We eat clover to get lucky and then shower and then shower, so as to cure the explosion of voices:

be the station, not the train. Be the station, not the train. Be the station-

ary, we fight back, *which migrates*.

When water seeps in, it reminds us movement (even in womb) is productive. It processes oceans. In waves.

Rodzina and *rodzice* is like saying *family* and *familites* (parents), which should be what we call them if they're more family than rent. They were twenty-three when they married, twenty-five when they had me, twenty-six when they immigrated to another country by themselves. Can you believe, and if you believe, can I believe your belief?

Grandm other other other   parent.

Bab cię cię cię

    you you you   *parent*[xviii]

Grandf ather doesn't face the same.

Caption:

My grandmother wears a knee-length dress at her wedding. It's mid-60's Poland; Communism rages, but so does fashion. The bones create a shadow pattern unique to her—a triangle, and, in the center, an eye—like a face fantasizes a new shape in the sun or old age. A bone, a face, each a fingerprint of stone, hardy until worn down. A halo rains light onto her shoulders, causing my grandfather, in black, to become a silhouette. Otherwise, jellyfish silk forewarns trouble. Her hands wrap in front of her belly, soon to be bella, her right hand confusing her left's fingers for stems. White, black, white flowers, line up like an organized crowd in bleachers, and their color, a dream. Her half-smile beads a number of emotions onto a tightrope that he'll confuse as material for tug-of-war. The etherealness of happiness and hope pull her further underwater. When she's pregnant, he leaves for a job abroad and again just before my mother's birth. He misses it, the totem his daughter rises to commemorate him. In this photograph, my grandmother is nineteen; my grandfather, twenty-two. I know him only as a good, kind man, severed from his past.

Grandm other other other sings a lullaby: *czerwona róża biały kwiat* about two young lovers who run into the woods because they grow tired of people judging their queer. They fall asleep, claiming the bird will wake them when it's time. I remember this song as being about death and absentmindedly type *czarna róża biały kwiat* into the search bar, sure the wet, dark pillow-throats of trees flush the rose

from rising.

The picture book flips to an easier ending:

a stationary man and stationary woman claim to love each other,
       anyway.

Yeah, right.

And the train? *Pociąg* where *po* means *after* and *ciąg, to pull*:

                    after pulling.

The train is only itself after arriving, unloading its freight.

The train is the station.

I cannot be that woman.

.

Parents file for a tourist visa on my be-half-bird multiple times. De-
clined, my dangerous, pending, noncommittal pendant status: a
shapeless oval shaping as it's spun or, rather, a gradually disappear-
ing ellipsis. Elapsed

elapsed

elapsed

on my mother's neck. Funny, when I think of it, I do not sexualize,
rather imagine it for torture. How I must have felt.

Of course your papers were declined. They knew you wouldn't have come back to the canary, carnation, incarceration, incarnation, incantation, inthenation, inhalation,

                                                            not then.

But now, travel holds me hostage.

It is my host, and my migrant bodies replicate within,
like a virus.

I want desire everywhere.

Not Paying for a Hotel Room After Midnight, Madrid Airport:

The seat divide keeps out the body that is at once whole and home-
less, so I quit the bench and retreat to the only place that's still

        lit, pick
a

stall and
   fall

asleep between two bodies, realizing there's nothing more comfort-
able with strangers than sleeping together where we can't afford a
country. In the lack of something, I nurse an impulse to never walk
a dog when it can walk itself. Never own a mug that says, *Meetings:
none of us is dumber than all of us*. Instead, remember borders exist
by attempting to cross them. Never off a domestic never-active to-do
list.

My grandmother says to my mother, *She gets her wandering eyes from you*. But she's a plant, she's a plant, she always tells me to grow roots and ceiling comforting.

Are you sure you're talking to the right daughter?

She has just one who won the lottery and began another memory, locked her wandering eyes in jars. The jars wandered away. Somewhere in the world, a museum has accepted their offer to attract motherlinear tourists and put them on display.

Here I am, a display of emotions colored by jet (generational) lag.

Now, sometimes I wear a lover over a book
        to sleep in order to develop
in reverse, be a child again, come
out from braiding language. *Cześć*, both hello and goodbye.
I'm begging you—
                I've been here too long—
tell me which one I'm on.

A bed, a lover, a dream, a place
        can be like that: force
                    me stay, yet help me leave.

Teenager of immigrant: I grow up to be transit or transistor, my phone shuffling consonants

or   continents.

I blame auto*correct* when it's wrong,

lose real-friend because becoming friends with friends is more permanent as transit. How I become friends with land transparent in transit. I find permanence only in smell.

When I sniff candles at the grocery store, memories are kind in them. I find Poland in a bouquet of churches and don't buy the one that's strong of love Mother in her black sweater because I don't want to own her

over the others

tongues[xix]

She wants her baby to like pizza, worries about birthday parties and school lunches, but it doesn't feel right to talk about pizza. It's never about pizza.

Memory: a child who caves attention stores it in a black hole re-
sistant to fire but susceptible to flooding, like the ponderosa pine.
Modified characteristics and smothered roots.

Allows the child to forget

      but remember the forgetting,

which sounds foreign because it's foraging,

      scavenging the empty space that a rose

can burn.

Sleeping on a couch downtown is a tantrum, a string of tantrums.

But I am not to make signals, only amplify them,

which is why I pour water for hours because water takes, it takes

time

to clean a wound that's across the water.

- *immigrant*: exotic
- *child of immigrant*: exception to subsequent points
- *teenager of immigrant*: neighborhood walks the neighborhood in a neighborhood stroller as if around a doll neighborhood
- *adult of immigrant*: ugly and deformed a neighborhood styled from the consecutive travels of one person the roofs sounding like barks because really they're rooves like missing grooves and whose on overworked hooves and hives and his

- *an excerpted child of exotic immigrants*: having been born in polepohleohlholeand and committed to America like a crime at age six now at age twenty-four I undulate between filling the hole and when I babysit it's not my baby it's not my baby it doesn't dare
- *immigrant of immigrant*: every traditional Polish name for a girl ends in a he's on and she's one always tagged with a always a abstinent a abducted ⬛ ey a beautiful oni a commanding I as ⬛
- *immigrant mot*⬛ I o o ⬛om my erotica because I ke⬛ ⬛language but promise I ca⬛ ⬛autocorrects to foreign a⬛ ⬛be it

- *child of im*⬛ Pierce) yes I would lo⬛ ⬛nspire just breathe I wa⬛
- *teenager of immigrant*: ⬛ transit ⬛ doesn't come through well on⬛ ⬛nsistor then OK yet sleeping on frie⬛ ⬛ is a tantrum a string of tantrums and you're not supposed ⬛ signal ⬛st amplify them
- *adult of immigrant*: raised as an imp for inopportune because I thought of that before impossible and as a result doesn't know how to deal with the
- *gimmick of rent*: to stay in one place is to

- *immigrandkid*: grandma's trying to explain where she's from and it's like explaining good to a child using only one-syllable words good is farm and town but not sit-tea is name but not my-name all love is good hug kiss sex heart the love good is bye
- *grand teenager*: grandma says yes OK fornicate but baby explain your abstinent language we are in need of more evolution
- *adult*: try I on the mend to make ion make electric couch of immigrant make tourist of immigrant yet cannot decipher between transit or transistor which would I rather be that's hard sit or stor

List(y) of People
Who Will Not Read This

i.

Loved children,

How does time take two months to finish kissing you at the airport? I don't take walks anymore. I don't have the time. Even when your father watches her, even when your brother, I don't attach to destinations, give to you and your brother. He returned from Germany on Saturday. Your daughter gave him a big kiss and called him *niuniu*. You see how she is. Children, I try my best to be a parent, but please let me know if you have any recommendations as to what I should give her or how I should act. She's thinning into quite the graceful child, yet slimming her further might take some time kissing as I don't want (her) to starve. We're in the city often, can buy all kinds of fruit, but her mood risks for a banana, and other times, she says *niecie*; oftentimes she uses this *niecie*. Listen, I purchase whatever I think she'll eat: a piece of chocolate, not too much, but however much fruit, and juices blended with old-boiled water. Your money holds strong, so don't send any dollars as long as she's healthy. She handles the road well, points out the window until someone finally answers *cow* or *that's a dog* with all the cows and all the dogs. R left for Germany, called a week later complaining about the conditions and pay. I helped K sort product for three hours and found a winter overcoat. For her, I gathered what fell in my hands, but they really didn't have much for children. To sum up the family visits, everyone thinks she's a well-behaved, smart, pretty girl, but you know that, and besides, your father has always called his granddaughter *naj-naj*.

Sincerely,

W

ii.

Dear fear,

Because of you, people christen scented paper and hand it next door for a wedding or a thank you. Nothing moves anymore. No one leaves the Midwest. No one closes a floor plan or keeps one's primary location—childhood—close. Dear fear, instead of I leave you, let me say I furnish you, in that I acknowledge your warmth, but also that you're the only thing that warms. A Polish immigrant must work so hard for the next generation, for *my* career. Too bad I'm an open floor plan, open to *I love you*. Let me acknowledge people's getting off on your sofa and other components of loyalty but also that you *want* to turn your room into something living roam, in that you're a supporter of writers but not a writer. What if this is me, too? Instead of I write my love, I love my writing, too. Fear, I know your type, these men who write about dying for women in a voice that sounds like they're not loving them. Prove to me you love me. Let me throw you a bone and teach you the word bone, so you can bring it back to me slick with saliva. You say, *Dear, we live in an uncle economy, where men like your father mess you up*, but I am a rock hard will / not. Instead of I love you, let me ask permission one last time.

Your doll,

Polalka

iii.

Loved children,

We're happy that life's not bad for you, as you say, and that you've finally bought yourself that car. Your brother jokes that you have the youngest one out of the whole family. Nothing is different here. The school year started and so did my old age. I signed up for twenty-three teaching hours because your father resigned from plumbing work here and there, but of course he won't dare resign from farming or sharing a small child. Renovation haunts the air next door. The plan is to paint the windows brown. My mother-in-law seems the most involved because she's the most worried about the outcome, and by this logic, I'm more involved in your life than you are. T returned from Iraq. He bought a Ford Sierra and is leaving for Germany to work as a welder, legally. N isn't planning to come back anytime soon. He's in California, told his mother on the phone it's a completely different world from Chicago. You're proud of your apartment but haven't sent pictures, so every day it recedes deeper in my unmemory. To end, I want to say that I have advanced from *baba* to *babcia* with my granddaughter, who hugs and kisses you fiercely.

Sincerely,

W

iv.

Iggy,

My mother begs me to write you because you live in America and have shits twice as big as mine. Seriously, that's why. Your mother doesn't want you to forget your heritage, and, well, you will sure as hell not forget me—heiritage, HA-HA. I can make American jokes. I'm a real boy! What, you don't think I'm familiar with Pinocchio? You're a rich boy for thinking that, a rich, real boy but not in spirit. *Może jesteś między złotem, ale nie jesteś złoty*. No, siiirupy. I think you're a big, fat, lying fake. Why'd you change Ignacy, your birth name, to Iggy, anyway? Is it because your choreless tongue tires or because you don't want your American friends to call you eye-nasty? S-o-u-n-d-i-t-o-u-t. Well, I bet you have boogers in your eyes, too. Tongue-tired boogers. I bet you can't even reach your nose to eat them, either. Or maybe you can and have dug a gargantuan nostril. Nostril-asshole. Hey, you know what I think? I lose track. My mother is making me write...I think Pinocchio is also a woman because your mother has got a nose on her. No, I mean she's got a lie on her, too. She made my mother believe that if I don't write these letters, we'll lose our place in the VISA line. Apparently she cuts the hair of a doctor who treats this man who IS a VISA. That's some messed up woman-Pinocchio bargaining. I have to remind you of Poland, or I won't inspire a chance to know anything besides. Maybe you're a nice kid. Maybe if we were brothers, we'd lie side by side, and between jerks of sleep, I'd entertain the thought of our being light pitter-patter rain, the one that doesn't hit you SO hard. But then we'd be in the same bed, safe and dry from the same rain. Write back if you dare.

Ignacy

V.

Grandma,

Colorado treats me well and gets me laid / back. Cats and dogs have eyebrows as long as the hair coming out of my head. Writing is scarce. I hold a pen's too-pink nose, and even though she lifts her chin to meet my intention, she flinches when it grazes. That's how writing is: scatce. I'm working on a cross / genre entry into poetry and writing to ask questions of water that's been left in the car. I could ask the phone but wish for distance from difficult questions and especially from the difficult person who asks them. Maturity plays into my ability to share this form with you, as I replace my parents at the other end of the line. Of course, parts of me do not extinguish, so you're bound to receive a puzzled (completed) version of them.

Say, these false ancestral selves may exist as my one clear self, changing, evolving, like there's a reason *pattern* arises from *parent*, *prenatal*. Don't tell your daughter about this correspondence. I'm crazy to protect her from a less private child than other children of parents. Protect you, too, but the removed name and ocean help, so feel free to refuse guard in your answers; I promise to stay guarded in my transfer of them to poetry, though I cannot promise to filter each word for the acceptance of masses, in both senses of the word. When I first took physics, I didn't believe in normal force, how it gives rise to masses, but now I think it's true. It takes normalcy. I'm not.

It's midnight now, and I'm standing outside the door to the difficult person who asks them, fumbling for the keys, listening to the washing machine rumbling rampage on the other side. Dangers of the night transpire there while I stand captivated by the stars. How's religion? How's the weather opposite of here? Or is that time? Do you remember my visa interview? Do you remember your first, your second, third trip to America? You were here for my first period, the first to know. Period. Somehow all of my firsts ran through your hands as your last firsts. A motherhood outlasting your own.

Your doll,

Polalka

vi.

Loved children,

Sometimes I worry that I am running out of time with her, but time is an endless horizon because she's only a child. She fits the sweater you sent her like water in a jar, and her other grandparents, too, though I don't like to admit it. They visited on Monday to drop off what you passed on through Aunt S. Thank you for the tights. I rip through mine domestically, so you hit the nail on the head. I found some photos of you and showed them to her. Right away she yelled, *Dad!* and only later recognized Mom. She asked me to pin them on the fridge, so I did. Oftentimes, when she points to them, she's really asking for you physically. She says Mom (*mamusia*) and Dad (*tatuś*) really nicely, shows others the photos, most frequently her best friend. It seems to me she forgets about you for a little and then suddenly revives her memory whenever she sees a plane, which is often these days. Other times she acts like a child with a radar for her parents, like a puppet you're playing from across the ocean. She's active and sometimes even restless. She'll spend the longest time flipping through picture books, asking a machine gun of questions. She doesn't like to spend time alone, although we've developed a routine where I place a book next to her as she takes her afternoon nap, and when she wakes up, she looks at it, patiently waiting for someone to get her. In these instances, she acts like an adult. No one knows what's on her mind lately. She's been making these momentary decisions. When we talk to the neighbors through the fence, she'll stand with me, she'll forget about you, she'll stand with me, but next thing I know, she's in their front yard, talking back. I'm remembering you asked what you should buy her, but I've recently purchased for her some everyday clothes: pants, long-sleeve shirts, tights. Now that I wash in the automatic, I need her to have clothes for a couple days at a time. Still sometimes she pees herself, and also it has turned to autumn.

Sincerely,

W

vii.

Eye-nasty,

How dare you send a flimsy button for luck and some instant coffee grounds that only stink up the envelope? You know it travels two long, wincing weeks to get to me, like an injured cat to the milk. Haven't you winter boots on your feet? OH RIGHT, you rehearse your poker face at dinner with your entire family—*here's how we don't show our cards.* Well, you know what doesn't stink up the envelope? Dollar bills. That new car smell. Hell, I'll even take an old car that craves some quitting-cigarette company: me and some goddam peace and quiet. I'll call it THROWN IGNACY. You know, there are six kids here, writing letters. We keep getting born because siblings need caretakers. OR friends, according to my mother, but she just needs God and somehow receives Him through our father. It's altogether odd how, in English, *be born* is a passive verb. I just learned that in school, where they tell us English is the universe. In Polish, it's just *urodzić się*. You do it. No one does it for you. Just like dying. Maybe that's where God comes in. He gives birth to American people—you're American now, so you tell me. It only seems that way from here, where everyone comes in at sundown—life's natural curfew—heats five spoonfuls of rice in a puddle of milk for supper, rubs off the shins with a sponge as surprisingly rough as hands recently ungloved, and then ventures upstairs to master some homework problem until one is caught-called to help the younger ducks do the same. I hear that, in America, you come home from school and do absolutely nothing. Just sit on your ass, smoke if you want. Throw your dick off schedule. You say in your letter that you eat pizza in a swimming pool, and I want to congratulate you on your grown-up behavior. Hey, since you're so grown-up, can you call Immigration Services and give them A BIG FUCK YOU?

Ignacy

viii.

Loved children,

Your daughter wants to move. I see it in the way she doesn't look behind her when crossing the road or in how she spends frivolously at the grocery store. Contrary to what she may think, you don't have much money. Continue to work hard as long as she's not on your clock. She's currently going through a *no* phase where everything is no. It's hard for her to even clean up her toys when she used to do it so well. Sometimes she says no before I say anything, and my hope is that this'll go away when she starts to understand whole sentences. But I am in awe of her logic. She comes up to me and says *opa*, meaning she wants me to take her in my arms, and when I tell her I have dirty hands, she says, *wash*. Sometimes when I challenge her logic, she smiles at me like a vice with qualifying documents, and when I silence her toys, I win their traits. I know you're waiting for pictures, but I'm afraid that none of them came out. I still have a few cages, so I'll try again and pass them on through Aunt S. Speaking of pictures, your father wants one of your car. He's driving me curious to ask. The situation in Poland isn't getting better. Newlyweds are learning it takes years to raise a worn out place where cars are numb, prices still rising. Your brother is at home. Doesn't know when B will return, so that he can take his place. He's running out of money, entering a national tragedy. There are no earning possibilities here. A from Połaniec came back for two weeks, says it's hard work for little pay and piss poor conditions. R bought a Fiat from J, bumped it in a week and completely totaled it in two. Your brother says it's a miracle he came out alive. V hasn't returned from the cucumbers. Apparently she met someone J whom she's bringing home to announce their engagement. You write that for an hour of work you can buy sixteen liters of gas. We can only buy two, but about sixteen liters of gum on her sneakers. We're happy that you're planning a visit, but maybe you can coordinate it with a wedding. In closing, I send you hugs and kisses.

Sincerely,

W

ix.

This letter is taken directly from the book, *Letters from Readers in the Polish American Press, 1902-1969* edited by Jaroszyńska-Kirchmann:

February 10, 1929, p. 17

Problem with Speaking

Garfield, N.J.—Dear readers of Ameryka-Echo!

My father is a reader of this newspaper and I am small but I know how to read and write in Polish because I go to a Polish people's school every Saturday. I was reading the newspaper Ameryka-Echo *and I noticed that a lot of Poles say that Poles are straightaway denationalizing themselves. I know why: because parents are uncaring and do not send their children to a real Polish school. And at home they do not talk as is proper. Poles talk like this: the dog is sitting and* waciuje hauzu *[is watching the house]; I was not in school because* waciowałem bejbki *[was watching the babies]; today for* diner *[dinner] I got* mit, potejty, kofi *[meat, potatoes, coffee] and* kiejksów *[cakes]; give me water, give me* naif *[knife];* Majk wysiajnuj *[Mike shine] my* siusy *[shoes], because I am going to a* mityng *[meeting]. Is this Polish speech? It isn't either in Polish or in English. And then they complain they don't know about whom. I would wish that in every city would rise a Polish People's Home and to send children there to school because in this school they teach the true history of Poland, not like in the Roman school: only a prayer and the catechism.*

W Gancarz

X.

Loved children,

We're sure she'll fly any day now. We cut her hair down to a boy's, so she'd have a lighter carry-on. I was going to let it grow, but after a couple of minutes entertaining her new pins, she took them out and refused to brush. Plus, everyone says she looks prettier this way. Your brother watched her while I was at church and reported that she handled herself better than he did, so we decided she was ready for marriage and bathrooms filled with botanical structure. He's been home since the wedding, chops wood and potatoes, has no idea when he'll be leaving next. Regarding potty training, I'll be honest, I can't keep up with how quickly she goes through cloth diapers, although at night, I use store-bought and plan to keep this going through winter. For the past week, she's been calling for the bathroom but is successful only 70% of the time and usually mistakes number one for number two. She likes to play dress up, shows everything to everyone, especially now that we have an automatic, and I can change her frequently to keep her clean. She's talking more and more, truly a smart girl. She gave the doctor a deep bow as a hello and didn't cry much during the shots but was in no mood to say goodbye. She weighs 14kg and is 88cm tall, which is close to the average for girls her age: 11.1kg and 81cm. What is your reaction to this? From what I can see, she's playful and active but really likes to look at books. My solution was to throw away the stroller, so now we take long walks in the afternoons over uneven terrain. She keeps calling for her *woziu* but is getting used to not having it, I think. I don't want to place her on a diet unless you come up with something reasonable because she's not overweight. That being said, I'll have to watch her closely because winter's coming. You ask about my health, and I can assure you I'm not dying until aliens inevitably wander Europe in English.

Sincerely,

W

xi.

Loosely addressed to Zygmunt Hertz, co-founder of Instytut Literacki, a Polish publishing house in France:

Publishing Sirs,

I ask about voice. It's something I need about years scissor-curling the spine because ever since we were children, as women, we were cut to be quiet with the pointer finger to both sets of lips. Our back holds no spine, but a rich axis around which we are spun, so I wonder if it's possible to raise girls without *shh* punt her away from certain deepest ways of communicating. Why didn't you have children? Were you afraid you'd hang their shade, qui(e)t them like the women in your letters whom you referenced only as rods on which your men hung their shade? You, as a man, weren't expected to breed or bread, but did you support your wife when she was called out, calls out? In English, son sounds like sun, but in Polish, *syn* sounds like sin or *sen*, which is dream. Were you afraid you'd have dotters? Instead, you called the publishing house your child. Did you publish your women as children, or did you not publish them at all? From over four-hundred-fifty titles published between 1946-1990, only thirty-some were authored by women, and mostly the same. There's something in need. When I say I grow up in the dirt, and he asks, *So is it unnatural to sit in a car at a stop-light?*, I laugh, but think it's not comfortable underwear; there's something I need under here. A *go*, a green light to manage my own affairs, a guise the shade of blood-crying or drooling, which is crying in reverse. I swear. Turn your face up-side down, and you'll drool right into your eyes. I apologize for your catcalling. I must have given the impression I possessed nine lives, which is the poetic thing about cats, but the poetic thing about me is that I have just one. Although I vow to love and respect a man, I do not vow to love your entity sirs.

Your doll,

Polalka

xii.

Great grandmother,

I'm in church about how I tell everyone you're still alive, ninety-something. I don't know; can that be right? A little less than twenty plus twenty plus twenty-five plus twenty-five. Everyone has kids young, and also my grandfather's the oldest, my mother's the oldest, and I'm the only.

You leave an astronomical presence in my childhood, a white, cratered Mars wrapped in an orange scarf, gossiping through the fence. Everyone speaks of your vigor. As long as you're milking cows and traveling to Germany on the Polish version of the Greyhound, you're going to live till you're a hundred, but as soon as you stop, you're going to live till whatever age you're at. I wonder how people measure my vigor. Maybe by how many cups of coffee I drink, but maybe that's my anti-vigor, my antidote.

The priest criticizes humankind's effort to build bomb shelters, rather than try to stop nuclear war, and by this logic, we should stop death, rather than live a safer existence. What do you think? Your survival is a phenomenon, although it probably isn't to you since you're the one living your alive. Have you stopped nuclear war or simply built bomb shelters? What's the better way to live than have kids young?

I want to buy a greeting card that says, *Congratulations, five generations of your family are alive at the same time.* It would celebrate both you and my future greeting-card baby. But time is running out, so, again, I'm asking what's better.

Great-grandma Fredzia, is being Fred-like why you never talk about the war? To appear ~~strong~~ manly? Why no one ever talks about the war, except for the quip about your husband's brother venturing to the school where they were keeping the Jews and getting shot at by mistake? Your son is a baby boomer, meaning you lived through it, and now there's Internet. Were we too far south? Catholic? So *badass*? Maybe it was a class thing, but we weren't rich. Or maybe everyone who was affected died with their memories as opposed to without.

Your doll,

Polalka

xiii.

Dear readers,

> "In Polish [when you're pregnant] you could be 'at/with
> hope' (przy nadziei), in an 'altered state' (w odmiennym st-
> anie), or in a 'blessed state' (w stanie błogosławionym)."
> (Oxford Dictionaries)

I would have named him Dominik, if he were a boy, she says with a smile that stretches goggles ear-to-ear. Their opaqueness grants her the ability to fake expression. She's thirty-two, still three short years from the child-bearing curfew she assigned her husband, but four years ahead of the ideal year, ninety-six, which would have been three from their first child, ninety-three, and two from the minimalistic twenty-six-year-old retirement from Poland and entrance into Chicago, ninety-four. The ideal year cleared almost peacefully but somehow began to exert more force once it passed, time-pushing my existence with winter windshield-wipers off her driving conditions. I bore you, reader, with years, but they're of peak importance. I become the not-product of a year. The wipers aren't whiskers, but her husband's and first child's fingers prying me off her vision. I would have been a boy—the past tense of an ideal year. I will be your future, whenever that may be.

Weak pitch by someone who's trying to get born, I know. But let me elaborate on how that ideal opportunity to enter the world was unjustly taken from me by a selfish daughter and a self-preserving, cautious husband, both of whom would never have matched my masterful native tongue.

In response to my mother's coo, the father says, *You know we can't have another child in America, with our daughter stewing in Poland.*

I know, my mother replies quietly and sighs, but from my casket of stillunborns (the more lively of the stills), I signal manically like a man-hand at a broken stoplight to point her to what she doesn't know: that I sleep on a waiting-room basket-bed weaved the moment of the mouth, that is, the moment she first spoke of a second glowing pumpkin ejecting from her warmth. They're moral to a fault, these people. They're driving to greet their daughter (my trapper) at O'Hare airport, a daughter who six-year stirred her grandparents' patience and did just that, stewed, in a Polish *garczek*, while her parents tried to *make it* in America. She spent time ignoring the more average and beneficial to me open seat in the melting pot.

I wish I could tell you this will be the first time they will see her since sealing her in a diaper (sealing, not trapping, in this case, for she has been able to breathe out pacifiers slobbered in complaints), but unfortunately, they were easily fooled and visited her every other summer, taking turns, sustaining injuries from the same copyright hearing: *I am an individual, and you may not reproduce (me).*

Of course, from a five-year-old, this sounded more like, *Come swing with me*, but with anger as my translator, the above rang true. The incorrigible game of telephone...

The father came away with minimal bruising to his foresight, but my mother's uterus spiked (spoke porcupine), meaning she would have popped any fetus like a happy birthday balloon, popped, not popped *out*. Their daughter's plea caused me to gag, gurgle, and invisible. My own injuries, unraveling from the central suffocation—this inability to be born—extended to my fingers, which were magician-gloved for the wait. The injuries cured them of their magic, or I'd have made her disappear. Instead, as I worked over-time as a traffic signal, I witnessed her wave an innocent glance at her parents and say, *You remind me of my parents.*

Now she enters view at the airport as a girly wiggle with a side ponytail. Hugging her parents into submission, even agreeing to have her picture taken beside her two large suitcases, she wanders ahead to sniff airport-lazy freshener and then the American air, which she complains smells more spoiled than its European counterpart. She may be smelling me, blemishing in my mother's juices; I hold on to dear life (not quite the word) in the ovaries, daring my egg to remain in a coma rather than push out the lips like a fatty piece of meat biting red lipstick. We have our own Day of the Dead here, and it comes every month more-or-less on date, a downpour staining a calendar through to the bottom. It's raining men; I know the agenda.

She waltzes into first grade continuing to sniff, all the while breaking her parents' cheerful expectations to have a child who prefers to stay in place; she didn't arrive soon enough for that. She smells of tent zippers and cooped-up reluctance, which will continue to hold its spoil fifteen years later as an effect of never giving up the heart of Europe, the desire to go back.

Her father will say, *We gave you everything you needed to succeed in this country, and you want to leave.*

And she will counter, *And I thank you for that, but I cannot stand routines and chain restaurants. I want to go back to Poland or at least Colorado, where I'll have mountains.*

She'll display minimal gratitude when she says this, not appreciating the luggage-in-wagon approach her parents were forced to take in greater America when they first landed their hands in the fortune race. She never even asked them about it, only heard trickles of story whenever she complained. If she didn't have it, they didn't have it in their basement, either. If she couldn't stand it, they couldn't stand next to it, or the bed, or the fridge, for they were contained in a tiny safety circle drawn in the sand. I would have been grateful and known their struggles. I would have been there, standing-baby on the windowsill.

But never mind the six years I lost while my trapper travelled Poland to further acquire her humanself. You, the reader, still mark my location three years away from curfew, and even though the wipers have thrown me onto highway lanes, I'm still visible.

I never do come alive (as you know by the plea). But why? Why am I not embryo-then-fetus feeling in her mother's renewed, dull uterus now that her daughter crossed the ocean? This time, the house-king strikes, fear on part of the father. He believes he is about to lose his job due to his company's forthcoming relocation to China and regularly replays his decline, *I'm living the American dream.*

We won't be financially stable enough to support another child. We will barely make it off my unemployment and your work, anyway, he says, emotionally restraining his wife. *It just won't work.* He repeats the word *work* to satisfy how unsteady of a job he has and how unsteady of a job another child would bring to the mix, an emphasis that offends me. I know my place may be as unnoticed as dawn's light on a wall, but in no manner do I think of myself as a job.

I know, his wife says and continues to measure her temperature every day when she wakes up to catch the four/tenths of a degree that would indicate ovulation.

On the eve of curfew year, when her husband finally gives in to her other plea to look into buying a house, he presents her with a choice. They moved from their basement to a two-bedroom condo in the suburbs and have been stewing there for five years, lacking a fireplace she associates with family-warmth. A big house has been her version of the American dream, and so when a house opens a few blocks from the apartment, she can't help but look. She tours the brick-built fireplace, the five bedrooms, five-and-a-half baths, and attempts to buy him over by offering office space, knowing well the self-importance of his intelligence. On the part of her intelligence, she assumes the space will basically have the child for her. *We don't need all this just for the three of us.* Remember, he has been on the brink of losing his job for three years, so it must be getting close.

He says, *You need to choose between the house and the child.*

She thinks about it, displaying hybrid unhappiness, *Well, maybe not the house... the kitchen floor...it's sticky...*

It's your choice, but if we do have another child, you'll be cleaning a lot more than a kitchen-floor spill of carbohydrate brains. Everyone knows what's coming, especially me, especially you.

They replace the floors. He does not lose his job for another eleven years.

I would like to conclude by no longer addressing my reader, but my writers. Karolina, you could have benefited substantially from my existence, learning interpersonal communication that would have turned your social life into a viable one, even after thick-processing through your deep-ended head. Instead of avoiding your roommates, hiding out in cafes, selfishly trying to make your unborn brother's voice come to life, a voice which you make mad in order to release his anger and free yourself from guilt, you would have been milking friendships, naturally tugging on people's resources. Father, you would have locked in another vote against romantic comedies. You would have felt less deleted from society's need for you, for your fatherness. And Mother, you would have known more than the losing whisper of your agreements.

The Son

xiv.

Poland beloved,

Instead of I leave you, say I love you because I have not yet matured enough to renounce my dual citizenship. I wonder what it would be like to lie in bed for the dream, where (it gets better) the lover's more than a disembodied glass Mr. Potato. Say I love you, yet you refuse my croaking and leave my neck-laced and brace / let you make this request at the typewriter, master—America, treat her fare well; she does me no good bye. Minnow, minnow, minnow it already looks like *little* and sounds like *cat*, so go ahead, call me minnow. My body's in love with what's unnecessary air; an extra space to breathe is maintaining distance while traveling with her shadowy radical or not doing anything when feeling all (potato). When you complain, we say, *Pick up (it gets) better.* You have been free since the eighties. Pick up the phone, trash, cat hairs stunning the surface of your coffee. You have to exist as other people for them, although your version of good is a central mother warmth, not wit, so you'd hate writing school; we try to wit ourselves out of anthologizing girls, also in the shower, but it feels good when it's banal. And it's easier to talk to a disembodied country about the personal because you'll put me in your (way) arsenal and reply condolences through amorphous television. I am not sorry this is also my father. It gets better than a stubborn toilet and writing school.

Your doll,

Polalka

P.S. If I returned, I'd be like, *Hi it's me hear me roar*, replying with amorphous television. All these years I am exposed to hunger. I'm hungry. Now you owe me a feast.

XV.

To Ignacy's daughter at 1-800-POLAND,

I found the letters your father sent long before I was born, and I'm wondering whether you exist and whether you're a product of resentment just as I am a product of guilt. My father's quiet about his childhood, says he never got the chance to meet your father. He never replied to his wedding invitation, the wedding I secured from the land before time. Sorry, I shouldn't mention American cartoons. It was a Polish wedding, complete with guitar and saxophone and that game where the bride collects everyone's loose change to finalize her position within the family bank. A wedding is definitely the time to come to America, at least that's what my extended family says about mine. I wonder how old you are. I recently became a woman because I 1) threw away those stuffies with magnetic limbs that cling to desolate chests. I hated the way I prodded their hands open with my grubby thumb, like the ocean prodded open our fathers; 2) planted my first chives and killed them, mad they weren't growing like so many things around them, like the world after a tragedy; 3) learned how to massage *myself*, which requires no explanation. Hey, do you have a favorite sound that means something in both languages? Mine is the letter ś because really you're saying, *shh*, and everyone gets mad at you for trying to be a teacher boss or something. I'll end with this: once, after a fight, my father asked, *We be good, ya?* But because he was muttering, I assumed he choked on some Polish word I didn't know, *łibiguja*. It's gibberish, of course, but ever since, it became our signal for everything is good, even if it isn't. So *łibiguja*, blondie, *łibiguja*.

Iggy's daughter

xvi.

Iggy,

You've got to help me silence the people in this town. They say I've killed my father because I cut my hair short and refuse to wear dresses. They think the devil's in me. I found your wedding invitation in a box of my father's old stuff, and you have to help me get to America. Please help me. That'll silence them, America wanting me. I don't know what's happening with my body, with my mind that's detached from it, but please know I will not survive here. Even my best friend, when she listens to me, doesn't really listen, comes off as more exterior than skin. Ever since the kids jumped her after her abortion and made her spray paint *murderer* in front of the church, she has no skin.

I just want to sit down and have coffee with my body.

I'll present two analogies here, but you only have to make it work with one. Do you know how, sometimes, you find a coin in the sand, and if you keep digging, you find another, and another, and it's like you've never been so rich? Well, finding these coins would be parts of me and another, but without my actually going to the beach, they slip further into the sand. Soon my body will be sunk in the wet part that no one likes to touch because it's been cooked with.

Okay, so do you also know it's nice to fuck before coffee? I don't know if you know because my father never mentioned whether you were friends like that. A fuck before coffee, when one of the two of you doesn't drink coffee is like a fuck before the rest of the day, too overwhelming. It's like that for me, except with an amorphous gender. A fuck before coffee when one of the two of you is too preoccupied with the meaning of fuck is like tackling the whole day before saying yes to your body.

You mentioned in a letter your mom knew someone or maybe still does, or maybe you do, but I don't know if you know since my father never mentioned whether you were friends.

Igancy's daughter

xvii.

Loved children,

I've been trying to reason how much to write about her because I don't want to cause any inadvertent missing. From the time your brother arrived home, she has taken to calling me *mom*, too, a word borrowed from the family library. She knows I'm Grandma, so she's simply braiding language. He left a week ago, not knowing if he'd have work. His pockets were empty. He even had to borrow from us for the road. He tried to quit smoking by busying his mouth with candy. Consequently, your daughter threw herself on sweets so diligently I first told him to eat his candy in peace and then just started rationing her. After a while, she returned to her norm. She really likes this Russian picture book I picked up from the library and tires us to death with her command, *Read to me*, the password for every moment. Your brother yells at me for sweeping in some Russian book as if it were a dead leaf. He can't read it nor imagine the stories like I do, but sometimes playing an instrument in Russian clears a cold room. Your daughter is such a bookworm. Your father says it's my fault, but I'm under the impression God zipped her into this disposition. *Grandma, read to me*. She's known for throwing up her hands and proclaiming, *Oh people people* or *Oh Jesus Jesus*. I was going to buy her a jacket but bought her a pea coat instead. It was expensive, but when your brother saw it, he said you two can afford a jacket *and* a pea coat, especially for All Saints Day. You bother me with your pains. I can ask that lady gynecologist for you, but, of course, if you need to go to the doctor sooner, don't hesitate. Money is important, but not the most. How are your ulcers? Are you treating them on your own or seeking medical help? For whatever reason, pessimism has whistled its way through this letter, and I am now very sad. I have to remind myself that she's our sun, and all I desire is for you to be well. She knows exactly where grandma's treasure is, pointing to my heart. To close, I end with strong kisses.

Sincerely,

W

xviii.

Grandma,

You sound like dharma, the nature or quality of *babcia*. You sound like *kapcia*, which means slipper—our family currency. You're always asking whether we're asking to get sick.

Grandma, I keep seeing your airport-face: hair and eyebrows darkened for my visit. You tell me I give you city-purpose, connected to all those years ago when you quit smoking because I was born. You bring me sandwiches for the ride home, but you say, *The water's warm; we stopped twice on the way to cool the engine.* We stop twice on the way back to cool the engine. I pee somewhere, not quite squatting on a grassed knee. You worry about the zooming that shakes our intention to eliminate my itch to flee. Already at eight I have this tic to ask if I'm going to make it through the night. This gives you city-purpose. You sit me down and say, *I get nervous too, can't sleep too, but you have to live inside a prayer.*

Grandma, would you accept me if I were to identify other than Mother? Other than the well behaved, smart, pretty girl you raised? Would you then understand my artistic capability? You were never able to figure out who I inherited.

Grandma, I bet you'd hate the end of the sentence in English because it insinuates there's time involved—period—whereas in our na(rra)tive tongue, it's just *kropka* or dot.

Grandma, when grandpa moves downstairs because his longs are no legger, why do you take his room? Why do you then move next door to his room and let your son renovate his room into a second kitchen where we eat holidays?

Grandma, I'm thinned to the lookings of a second kitchen. Grandma, I have so much to say, but it's all coming out like this. I'm already sick.

Your doll,

Polalka

xix.

This letter is in response to the letter to the editor, *Problem with Speaking:*

Dear letter to the editor,

Imagine my trying to find the people in this world in whose memory you exist, residents of New Jersey or someplace already better traveled. If I approached them for an interview, they'd say, *Leave me alone* faster than the word for grandfather in Polish, *dziadziu*, which thaws the same spoiled sound as *dziki* (wild) and *dzidziuś* (baby)—not meant to be pronounced by the foreign-born. Unless, of course, I interrogated your grandchildren in Polish, in which case we would both repeat your name, botching it at various degrees, and accomplish nothing. No one remembers how to speak Polish outside of Polish names anymore.

TV show idea: detectives tracking down people with pleasant memories of criminals and treating them like criminals.

My search for you online fails. I even sign up for MyHeritage.com to pretend I have a memory, but the website produces x out of five stars under each listing, as if this actually were a TV show, which upsets my efforts beyond revival. All the Władysław Gancarzs have three out of five stars and die at death place and are buried at burial place.

Reaching back into your letter, I want to attend to the phrase, *America echoes.* Who exactly is speaking, and where is the sound reflected? It has come to my attention that *Ameryka-Echo!* is a publication for Polish immigrants in America, so does it have the audacity to say immigrants move America to imitation? Or is the hyphen simply a comma: America, we command you to Echo! your role, so we can follow it?

Additionally, the syntax in your letter is atrocious, and because I know the letters originally appeared in Polish, I wish to track down your translator and kick his formalities into a discussion about how ridiculously they mock a letter about improper Polish speech and its attack on nationalism.

However, I am intimate with your content because I experience it, too. When I was young, I was the only one who answered to purebred spoken Polish with chopped language, as if the creases on my tongue actually meant something. Now my parents, Americanized, do it too. Ponglish triumphs over every interaction. We never speak a sentence in either Polish or English, but both, and sometimes, neither; an English verb will cater to a Polish ending, an English noun will fall to a Polish pronunciation, and vice versa. In Poland, the words *okay* and *good* and *love* replace their Polish counterparts.

What I mean to say is, what is a dry teabag except for a satchel containing dead grass and that grass possessing an intrinsic quality of being easily transformed by a flood of water at once? Then a wet teabag is no longer known to us as an organizing principle but a single unit of wet rat or mole uncurling in the palm. Immigrants to America are satchels containing dead language, and that language possesses an intrinsic quality of being easily transformed by the ocean. Then a wet immigrant, no longer capable of organizing it into separate grains, together with both languages, becomes nation vermin.

Then I ask: can we ratify a teabag with tears?

Your doll,

Polalka

Glossary

babcia vs. *baba:* both mean grandma, but the former is definitely the more polite, delicate term. The latter suggests Baba Jaga (Baba Yaga in Russian), a mythical, mean old witch

biały orzeł: white eagle

cię: you, but only when it follows a verb, such as *kocham* cię (I love you)

czerwona róża biały kwiat as opposed to *czarna róża biały kwiat*: the former says red rose white flower, while the latter morphs to black rose white flower

dzieńdobry: the literal translation is day good, but people utter this for the sentiment of good morning or good afternoon, or even hello

Dziennik Związkowy: the newspaper my parents flipped through for the newest Visa Bulletins

hasło: password. I place it here because of the word's auditory resemblance to house

i: and

i ty: and you

jutro wariaty sosna lipy: tomorrow idiots aspen lindens

istnienie: existence

listy: snail-mail letters

naj-naj: naj is a prefix attached to words that means most. The best translation of this nickname would be most-most

nie: no

niecie: a short, whiny version of the word, *niechce*, which means I don't want

niuniu: this nickname doesn't necessarily have a basis in the Polish language. Uncle is *wujek,* in-short, *wuju.* I might have taken this shortened term and ran with it

obwarzanka: street bread that's boiled before it's baked and usually sprinkled with poppy or sesame seeds. It can be found in many carts throughout larger cities in Poland and sells as easily as popcorn or sugared nuts in the States

on / ona / oni: he, her, they

pan: man

Polalka: a composite of Polish & *lalka* (doll)

prosie: pig

prosze: please

rodzice: parents

rodzina: family

sen: dream

syn: son

ten: this, usually followed by a noun

tęsknota: the noun that corresponds to the verb to miss (someone), which doesn't enjoy a counterpart in English. The closest are longing and nostalgia, but nothing in them is missing

ufam ci: I trust you

wina: fault

woziu: a cuter version of saying *wózek*, or stroller

zdychają & umierają: the former is a common term used when animals die, while the latter signifies the death of a human and can be considered a euphemism for dying

żona: wife, although it's very familiar to the English, zone

Sources

Meena Alexander, *The Poetics of Dislocation*

Anna D. Jaroszyńska-Kirchmann, *Letters from Readers in the Polish American Press, 1902-1969*

Anne Carson, *Nox*

Hélène Cixous, *Stigmata: Escaping Texts*

CA Conrad, *A Beautiful Marsupial Afternoon*

Ching-In Chen, *The Heart's Traffic*

Clarice Lispector, *The Hour of the Star*

Danielle Dutton, *Here Comes Kitty*

DC Eagle Cam http://www.dceaglecam.org/

immihelp.com, "Proof of Family Relationship: I-130 Petition - Family Based Green Card & Bona Fide Marriage Documentation" (italics are my own)

J'Lyn Chapman, *Beastlife*

Bob Hicok, *Plus Shipping*

Justin Nobel, "Rare White Eagle Stirs Souls," Audubon.org

Michelle Naka Pierce, *Continuous Frieze Bordering Red*

Official Website of the Department of Homeland Security - U.S. Citizenship and Immigration Services, "Bringing Parents to Live in the United States as Permanent Residents"

reddit.com, "Genderqueer" https://www.reddit.com/r/genderqueer/comments/47rtjp/if_anybody_could_help/?st=it0qx6lq&sh=c26e6454

Richard M. Stana, Evi L. Rezmovic, "Immigration Benefits: Several Factors Impede Timeliness of Application Processing"

Susan Sontag, *As Consciousness Is Harnessed to Flesh*

United States Department of State Bureau of Consular Affairs, "Visa Bulletin - Immigrant Numbers for June 1999," "Visa Bulletin for March 2017"

visajourney.com, *I-130 FAQs* (italics are my own)

Zofia Reych, "A Polish abortion ban would turn women back into childbearing instruments," *The Guardian*

The letters from W are actual letters written by my grandmother and sent to my parents during the six years I lived with her in Poland. I took the liberty of translating them and being playful with the language.

Acknowledgements

I want to thank my grandparents to whom I am eternally grateful for inviting me into their home and heart. Dziękuje za opieke nad moją myślową głowę.

I want to thank my parents, my forever-support-system, role models, and best friends.

I want to thank Michelle Naka Pierce, whose book *Continuous Frieze Bordering Red* inspired this project. J'Lyn Chapman who oversaw the writing of this book from start to finish and offered sage cutting advice, so I wouldn't end up with a 200-pg encyclopedia on all-things-Poland. Other instructors and friends at Naropa University, including but not limited to Jeffrey Pethybridge, Sarah Richards Graba, Andrew Schelling, Serena Chopra, Anne Waldman, Julie Carr, Brenda Coultas, TC Tolbert, and CA Conrad.

Thank you to Jack Kerouac School cohorts of 2016, 2017, and 2018, for providing endless inspiration in the classroom, around bonfires, and through parking lots. Special thanks to Margaret Bryant, Megan Heise, Shawnie Hamer, Jenni Ashby, Gabrielle Lessans, Dani Ferrara, Heather Fester, Caitlin Berve, Marie Conlan, Swanee Astrid, Aisling Daly, Travis Klempan, Shelly Robinson, Sarah Escue, Emily Duffy, Eric Shoemaker, Kristiane Weeks Rogers, and Kaleb Worst.

Thank you to Ryan Mihaly who is a faithful editor, talented writer, and translator. He has lovingly collaged the cover for this book.

Thank you to Adam Levin who was a big part of my life during this time. Jessica Gudel, Caerlina Williams, Kaela Hendricksen, and Olga Bednarek for always providing a heart-home upon my return. And Sarah Engler, Esha Mehta, Bella, and Dragon for believing in my being able to pay rent as a poet.

And thank you to the editors at Spuyten Duyvil who worked tirelessly to give these words a context and the context, a frame.

KAROLINA ZAPAL is an itinerant poet, essayist, and translator. Her work has appeared in The Manhattanville Review, Bone Bouquet, Foglifter, Witness, Bombay Gin, and others. She served as the Anselm Hollo Fellow at Naropa University from 2015-2017. She's an editor with The Birds We Piled Loosely Press and an appointed Bridge Guard in Štúrovo, Slovakia. Born in Poland and raised in the United States, she wonders about lost cities and impenetrable borders. This is her first book. Her website is karolinazapal.com.

CPSIA information can be obtained
at www.ICGtesting.com
Printed in the USA
BVHW052114281220
596438BV00003B/82